Head

THE MUSICAL

Book, Lyrics, and Music by

Debbie Patterson

*Head*
first published 2007 by
Scirocco Drama
An imprint of J. Gordon Shillingford Publishing Inc.


Scirocco Drama Editor: Glenda MacFarlane
Cover design by Terry Gallagher/Doowah Design Inc.
Cover and production photos by Allen Fraser
Printed and bound in Canada

We acknowledge the financial support of the Manitoba Arts Council, The Canada Council for the Arts and the Government of Canada through the Book Publishing Industry Development Program (BPIDP) for our publishing program.


Production inquiries should be addressed to:
Debbie Patterson
166 Chestnut Street
Winnipeg, MB R3G 1R6

Library and Archives Canada Cataloguing in Publication

Patterson, Debbie, 1966-
Head/Debbie Patterson.

A play.
ISBN 978-1-897289-18-1

1. Anne Boleyn, Queen, consort of Henry VIII, King of England, 1507–1536—Drama. I. Title.

PS8631.A8465H42 2007 C812′.6 C2007-901644-8

J. Gordon Shillingford Publishing
P.O. Box 86, RPO Corydon Avenue, Winnipeg, MB Canada R3M 3S3

# Acknowledgements

Development of this play was nurtured by Shakespeare in the Ruins with generous support from the Winnipeg Arts Council New Creations Program.

Dramaturgical support was generously provided by Shakespeare in the Ruins, the Manitoba Association of Playwrights and Playwrights Workshop Montreal. These organizations supported a series of workshops and readings which allowed the script to grow into its present form. Thanks, too, to the actors who breathed life into these words: Paulina Abarca, Graham Ashmore, Mairi Babb, Michelle Boulet, Sarah Constible, Eric Davis, Paula Jean Hixson, Marcel Jeannin, Helen King, Kevin Klassen, Nadine Gilroy, Carolyn Gray, Rob McLaughlin, Wayne Nicklas, Csilla Przibislawsky, Marina Stephenson Kerr, Laura Teasdale, and Melanie Whyte. Thanks also to Rick Chafe, Emma Tibaldo, Glenn Buhr, Dr. Phillip Hall, Rory Runnells, Stephen Lawson, Margaret Sweatman, Ross MacMillan, Terésa Lee, Kathleen Hull and Marv Terhoch.

For guidance, inspiration and encouragement, thanks go to Brian Drader, whose dramaturgy was instrumental in this script's development.

But above all, thanks to Arne MacPherson for his unstinting praise, limitless patience and grace.

Financial assistance to support the writing of this play was generously provided by the Manitoba Arts Council and the Winnipeg Arts Council.

## Characters

King Henry VIII
Anne Boleyn: ............... Queen of England,
second wife of King Henry VIII.
Thomas Cranmer: ....... the Archbishop of Canterbury.
Kingston: ....................... warden of the Tower of London.
Lady Kingston: ............ aunt of Jane Seymour,
wife of Lord Kingston.
Jane Seymour: ............. future wife of King Henry VIII.
Fool: .............................. Anne's female fool.
Mistress Stoner: ........... menial labourer at the Tower of London.
Mark Smeaton: ............ Anne Boleyn's musician.
Officer/Sirrah/Lord Norfolk

## Setting

London, England. Spring, 1536.

## Production Information

*Head* was commissioned and first performed by Shakespeare in the Ruins at the Assiniboine Park Conservatory, on September 14, 2006 with the following cast:

ANNE BOLEYN .......................... Marina Stephenson Kerr
LADY KINGSTON ........................................ Miriam Smith
JANE SEYMOUR ......................................... Samantha Hill
FOOL ............................................................... Nancy Drake
MISTRESS STONER ....................................Melanie Whyte
HENRY VIII .........................................................Cory Wojcik
LORD KINGSTON ...................................... Steven Ratzlaff
THOMAS CRANMER ................................. Richard Hurst
MARK SMEATON/OFFICER/SIRRAH .. James Johnston
MUSICIANS ..... Karen Erhardt, Greg Lowe, Erica Schultz

Directed by Arne MacPherson
Designed by Brian Perchaluk and Eric Bossé
Music composed by Debbie Patterson
Music arrangements and direction by Greg Lowe
Vocal direction by Pat Rabson
Choreography by Kimberly Rampersad
Stage Managed by Georgette Nairn and Allison Loat

## Debbie Patterson

Debbie Patterson is a Winnipeg actor, playwright, composer and musician. She studied acting at the National Theatre School of Canada, is a founding member of Shakespeare in the Ruins and the former Artistic Director of the Popular Theatre Alliance of Manitoba. Her other plays include two one-woman shows: *Pandora's Squeezebox: a sex love power pleasure cabaret*, and *Wide Open Beaver: Uncut Canadian Content* as well as *Candy From a Baby*, which won Best of the Fest at the 2006 Winnipeg Fringe. She lives in Winnipeg with her fabulous family: partner Arne MacPherson and their two children Gislina and Solmund.

# Act One

## Scene 1: A Party in the Palace

*Sumptuous music swells and the courtiers enter and sing.*

***The Most Happy***

LADIES: Pretty ladies dancing so sweetly,
Butterflies flitting, flirting discreetly,
Light as a melody floating on air:
Pretty ladies everywhere.

GENTS: Happy ladies laughing together,
Bouquets of beauties blooming forever.
Laughter their perfume sweetens the air:
Happy ladies everywhere.

ALL: But the most happy lady's the lady who's queen,
The envy of courtiers, every girl's dream:
Radiant, brilliant, the star of the land!
The most happy lady is Anne!

*ANNE and HENRY enter. They are not happy. He deposits her unceremoniously in her chair and turns abruptly. She holds him back, he rebukes her, she kisses his ring daring him to dismiss her, he leaves her.*

See her enter the room on the arm of the king,
See the love in his eyes as she kisses his ring!
A husband so gentle, a lady so mild,
But alas, no male child.
We can see the affection between these two:
The glow of their true hearts shining through;

Their love would sustain through joy and despair
If the queen could produce an heir.
But the most happy lady's the lady who's queen,
The envy of courtiers, every girl's dream:
Radiant, brilliant, the star of the land!
The most happy lady is Anne!

ANNE: In the beginning I was happy.
How could such joy become despair?
My heart was safe in Henry's love;
My body rich with England's heir.
But I've miscarried of my saviour:
My charming prince is dead and will not come,
I shan't be rescued by a miracle;
My body has failed and failed and failed to birth a son.

HENRY: Pretty ladies dancing so sweetly,
Butterflies flitting, flirting discreetly,
Light as a melody floating on air:
Pretty ladies everywhere.

ALL: Happy ladies laughing together,
Bouquets of beauties blooming forever.
Laughter, their perfume, sweetens the air:
Happy ladies everywhere.
But the most happy lady's the lady who's queen,
The envy of courtiers, every girl's dream:
Which one will it be, to share the king's bed,
If the old queen should lose her head?

*The song ends and the ladies and gentlemen applaud politely. JANE SEYMOUR and LADY KINGSTON are together. HENRY approaches JANE.*

JANE SEYMOUR: He's coming.

LADY KINGSTON: Of course.

JANE SEYMOUR: He will ask me to dance.

Samantha Hill (Jane Seymour)

LADY KINGSTON: And you will refuse.

JANE SEYMOUR: What?

LADY KINGSTON: Let me have at him first. Trust me.

HENRY: Good evening my dear Mistress Seymour.

JANE SEYMOUR: Your majesty.

*She curtsies and he kisses her hand. Slowly.*

JANE SEYMOUR: Heavens.

*LADY KINGSTON clears her throat and HENRY breaks away reluctantly.*

HENRY: And my dear Lady Kingston.

LADY KINGSTON: At your service.

HENRY: Indeed.

LADY KINGSTON: How delightful to see the Queen once again amongst society. She has recovered from her…mishap?

HENRY: Yes, Lady Kingston, but her physician advises her to refrain from dancing. I, however, would be dancing to these refrains. My wife is of no use to me and so I would speak with your truly radiant niece.

LADY KINGSTON: With my blessing.

HENRY: Mistress Seymour, would you do your King the honour?

*He bows and extends his hand.*

LADY KINGSTON: Mistress Seymour, are you faint?

JANE SEYMOUR: Heavens.

*She swoons and relaxes into HENRY's arms with a sigh. He helps her gently onto a seat.*

HENRY: God in heaven! You sweet little bird.

LADY KINGSTON: You must forgive her. We've only just arrived and my poor niece must have a few minutes to catch her breath.

JANE SEYMOUR: Then I require you to dance in my stead.

LADY KINGSTON: What?! Oh no, I couldn't.

JANE SEYMOUR: I insist. Your majesty, you came to us in search of a partner for a dance and I would not fail to satisfy your desire.

HENRY: Oh, no no no…

JANE SEYMOUR: I beg you, dance with my Aunt.

LADY KINGSTON: Really!

HENRY: Of course. Lady Kingston? Would you—

LADY KINGSTON: I can refuse you nothing.

HENRY: Come.

*He leads her on to the dance floor and signals to the band to begin playing. MARK SMEATON plays the recorder. They dance.*

LADY KINGSTON: I am sorry, sir, that your wife is of no use to you, but delighted that I may be of service. I do so love to dance.

HENRY: Your niece is lovely.

LADY KINGSTON: Yes, isn't she? And I dare say your queen is looking quite fit. Such a tragedy. To lose a boy after you've waited so long and borne such trials—

HENRY: Yes, thank you.

LADY KINGSTON: But you needn't bear these griefs alone, your majesty. The nation shoulders the burden with you: we've all lost an heir in your queen's misfortune. Poor Jane has been inconsolable since your loss. She's quite anxious to be a mother herself.

HENRY: But she's not yet married.

LADY KINGSTON: No.

HENRY: Is she promised to anyone?

LADY KINGSTON: No, your grace. She is very much available.

HENRY: Mmmm...

LADY KINGSTON: I shall always be grateful to your majesty for the care you took to arrange my marriage to Lord Kingston.

HENRY: Yes?

LADY KINGSTON: As wife to the Warden of the Tower of London you've blessed me with a title and meaningful occupation: a rare gift for a woman. My niece would be honoured if you would consider extending the same care to her.

HENRY: She wants a husband?

LADY KINGSTON: To be quite frank, marriage is not foremost in her mind.

HENRY: She wants a lover?

LADY KINGSTON: Heavens! She wants children! She aches to be a mother. The fairer sex cannot take to the battlefield as men may do, yet like a lusty, young soldier she longs lay down her body to serve king and country: by bearing children. As our queen has tried so valiantly to do.

HENRY: Let us pray that your niece is a better soldier than the queen.

LADY KINGSTON: The curse of barrenness has never afflicted a woman of her blood. God has seen fit to bless her with four fine brothers and many uncles, healthy handsome gentlemen all. Your wife also has one brother. She may yet bear you a son.

HENRY: I will have no more boys by her.

LADY KINGSTON: Still, I pray that the queen might yet conceive.

HENRY: She shall not by me.

LADY KINGSTON: Indeed, not by you.

*They dance while SMEATON sings.*

***Sweet Rose***

SMEATON: *(Singing.)*
So tenderly music caressed her body,
Our spirits twain, entwined in the air,
Her breast enfolded in sweet melody,
Her rapture all my care.
*Singing lully lully lully (etc.)*

*SMEATON's singing continues under the dialogue.*

LADY KINGSTON: You enjoy this music, my lord?

HENRY: His singing is impeccable.

LADY KINGSTON: But he plays with his privilege. And though he holds the rhythm, he forgets his place.

HENRY: Is Master Smeaton becoming ambitious?

LADY KINGSTON: Look how he eyes your wife.

SMEATON: *(Singing.)*
Sweet rose, fair flower all unregarded,
Plucked in the prime and left to fade,
By gardener proud and empty-hearted!
O, had I your rich bed made.
*Singing lully lully lully (etc.)*

LADY KINGSTON: Are you quite sure the queen's last debacle was of your blood?

HENRY: You forget your place.

LADY KINGSTON: I spoke with the gravedigger who buried the thing. "Scarcely human," he said.

HENRY: Test not my charity!

LADY KINGSTON: I dare not believe such issue could be of royal blood.

HENRY: Hush! Go gossip with your cronies.

SMEATON: So tenderly took I up that flower.
Her scent my senses vanquished,
Thus drained of all my manly power
Wrapped in her arms I languished.
*Singing lully lully (etc.)*

HENRY: This song grows irksome.

LADY KINGSTON: It may be merely gossip, my lord, it may well be.

HENRY: What have you heard?

LADY KINGSTON: I would not, for all the world, abuse your ear with these vile—

HENRY: Out with it. Now! What have you heard?

LADY KINGSTON: Forgive me, but some say—

HENRY: Who? Who says—

LADY KINGSTON: It is widely believed that the queen has become rather too familiar with certain gentlemen. Indeed, it has gone so far that many fear…

HENRY: What?

LADY KINGSTON: If, as you say, the queen will have no more boys by you, then by whom? Will England's crown be passed down to the bastard son of some smirking privy counselor, or worse? Forgive me, your grace. This news comes hard.

HENRY: Harder for you, madam, and the gossip mongers who noise such slanders about my court.

LADY KINGSTON: Forgive me your grace, but I believe—

HENRY: Lies! You believe treasonous lies! And repeat them like the foul traitor you are.

LADY KINGSTON: I hardly dare to speak such things, and yet silence makes me complicit in their treasons. My honest concern for your grace urges me—

HENRY: I am not a cuckold! Do you see horns upon my brow?

LADY KINGSTON: A crown of thorns was set in mockery upon our Saviour's brow, yet that insult survives as a symbol of His grace, of His great sacrifice. It may be that such bitter medicine is required to heal your ailing nation. The queen is no favourite of the people and God has not blessed her with a son. What if you were free to marry another: one milder, more obedient. One who will bear you sons aplenty. What a gift that would be to the people of England. Only a truly great king could suffer so for his nation. You would be our saviour.

HENRY: If you are wrong you shall pay dearly for it.

LADY KINGSTON: And yet I pray that I am wrong, for your grace's dignity.

*Pause.*

HENRY: I shall launch a formal investigation into the queen's affairs.

LADY KINGSTON: A wise move.

HENRY: Once sufficient cause is discovered I shall have her

imprisoned at the tower. You will attend her and report her every word to me.

LADY KINGSTON: Certainly.

HENRY: I want a confession.

LADY KINGSTON: I shall do my utmost—

HENRY: Get a witness: another lady to attend her, to verify your reports.

LADY KINGSTON: Don't you trust me?

HENRY: I will not have the veracity of your reports called into question.

LADY KINGSTON: As you wish.

HENRY: Her guilt will be beyond all doubt.

LADY KINGSTON: I shall dedicate myself to your service in this matter.

HENRY: And I shall handsomely reward your efforts.

*The song draws to a close.*

LADY KINGSTON: The measure is ending and I must surrender you to my niece. She looks to be well enough to dance.

HENRY: She is lovely.

*They curtsy to one another.*

LADY KINGSTON: And she'll give her husband lovely babies.

HENRY: Yes, she will.

*As the people applaud the music, HENRY crosses to JANE, he takes her hand and whispers to her. She whispers back and he touches her. ANNE stands to protest but HENRY thwarts her.*

HENRY: The queen will now retire to her chamber. We

thank her for her presence but must not tax her delicate condition by suffering her to remain with us any longer.

ANNE: I thank your grace for your loving kindness, but—

HENRY: Show her your love!

*He initiates applause for ANNE.*

ANNE: Spare me your love, I have no desire to leave.

HENRY: The queen is a lusty wench: hale and hearty as a soldier. No wonder she cannot give us a son; she hoards her manly fortitude for her own use.

*The crowd laughs.*

Come, madam, deport yourself as a Lady should.

ANNE: *(To HENRY alone.)* That shall I, when my husband deports himself as a gentleman.

HENRY: *(To ANNE.)* Out of my sight! *(To the crowd.)* The queen takes her leave. Show her your duty.

*The courtiers begin to curtsy and bow.*

ANNE: Come, Ladies.

HENRY: Stay, Ladies. The gentlemen here need your company. Take your Fool.

ANNE: Very well.

*With a look ANNE tells the courtiers to bow to her.*

I thank you for your loves. I am loath to leave such a beautiful assembly. But though I must perforce remove my person, I pray you hold me here in your hearts. Ladies, remember your queen as you dance with her husband.

HENRY: Good night, my queen.

*ANNE and the FOOL exit.*

HENRY: And now, play music! And dance, lusty gentlemen! *(Privately.)* Lady Kingston, you will prepare the queen's chambers at the Tower immediately against her possible stay there. I intend to move swiftly in this business and I would not have the queen accommodated unsuitably.

LADY KINGSTON: I am your servant.

HENRY: Dance! Dance!!

*HENRY dances with JANE, LADY and LORD KINGSTON dance. The band sings a round of "The Most Happy" as a drunken chorus.*

**Scene 2: Anne's Chamber**

*FOOL enters with her baggage. She is moving on.*

FOOL: There's not a fool so simple but she can tell which way the wind blows.

*The FOOL approaches the door, stops herself. She can't leave. MARK SMEATON enters with his bags, perhaps an instrument.*

Master Smeaton, are you off too?

SMEATON: Summoned by his majesty, himself!

FOOL: Summoned?

SMEATON: By his majesty!

FOOL: Are you to enter his service?

SMEATON: That is my hope. At the revels on Tuesday last he made good note of me. But I dare not be so bold as to hope for—

*JANE SEYMOUR enters with her bags. Sees the FOOL and SMEATON ready to leave.*

JANE: Even the entertainers are abandoning her. You're wise to do so: naught but ill will come to the queen, I fear. Farewell.

*JANE exits.*

SMEATON: Where are you going?

FOOL: I don't know.

SMEATON: Come with me to the king, I'll petition him on your behalf.

FOOL: No. I thank you, but no.

SMEATON: Fare you well, then.

*MARK SMEATON exits. The FOOL sings.*

***The Fool's Song***

FOOL:
What?
What would you do?
If someone depended on you but you knew
There was nothing you could do…
What?
What would you say?
If you'd been her fool for seven years
Would you stay her fool for one more day?

Like rats from a sinking ship
I've watched them all scurry off to safety.
I'm the only one who hasn't turned tail,
It's time I faced the reality:
That the queen's not long for her crown,
There are some who would bring her down,
And no one knows which way the tree will fall.
Now it seems my choice is a simple one,
Stand my ground or turn and run.
Safety waits outside that door, so why do I stall?

Run, Fool, run!
Feet carry me away.

Don't listen to the heart beating
Stay, Fool, stay!

If I run, I'm a rat like the rest of them,
Letting fear and suspicion rule,
But courage and oblivion have always been
The modus operandi of the fool.
To abandon her, I must betray myself
I am not what I am if I flee,
But the queen has one foot on a banana peel:
When it all falls out, the joke could be on me!

Run, Fool, run!
Feet carry me away.
Don't listen to the heart beating
Stay, Fool, stay!
I cannot run, I cannot stay.

ANNE: *(Off stage.)* Fool?

FOOL: *(Thinking fast.)* Uhhh… Madam?

*ANNE enters.*

ANNE: Fool, I— *(She stops, takes in the almost empty room.)* This is a strange sight.

FOOL: A solitary fool.

ANNE: Where are my gentlewomen? *(The FOOL shrugs.)* They should be here to accompany me to chapel. Where are they?

FOOL: Gone?

ANNE: Something's amiss—

FOOL: I smell it on the wind.

ANNE: —In fear of which I dare not miss a chance to kneel in prayer.

FOOL: Then hie you to the chapel.

ANNE: I cannot go to chapel with a solitary Fool. I must have my ladies with me.

FOOL: A lowborn country servant maid may go to chapel when and with whom she pleases, but a queen must sit shut up in her royal station like a statue, static in her status…

ANNE: Where are my gentlewomen, Fool?

FOOL: They have fled, madam.

ANNE: All?

FOOL: All. And Master Smeaton besides.

ANNE: Fled.

FOOL: And therefore, madam, I beg leave to be released from my obligations to your grace. I fear some danger to my person if I stay.

ANNE: Why? What is going on?

FOOL: I know not, but if I stay I will find out. In such cases the wise embrace ignorance and fly.

ANNE: What, would you leave me all alone?

FOOL: Please.

ANNE: And where would you go? Who do you have besides myself?

FOOL: Who do you have besides myself?

ANNE: If you loved me you would stay.

FOOL: Madam—

ANNE: Stay with me Fool. No harm will come to you, I swear. I will protect you.

FOOL: And if you cannot?

ANNE: I need you.

*An OFFICER enters.*

OFFICER: Forgive me madam. I regret I must convey you to the Tower.

ANNE: On what business?

OFFICER: I know not.

ANNE: Silly Fool, my household has merely been moved without my knowledge, that's all—

*The OFFICER holds out wrist irons. ANNE freezes.*

OFFICER: Madam?

FOOL: Madam, you are arrested.

ANNE: I am to be your prisoner?

OFFICER: That is my charge, your highness.

ANNE: I have committed no crime.

OFFICER: I have no knowledge of your charge.

ANNE: Then you have no reason to convey me hence.

OFFICER: I have my orders.

ANNE: You are out of order.

FOOL: Who has ordered the queen's arrest?

OFFICER: I know not.

ANNE: This is madness.

OFFICER: All I know is that I'm to come here, put you in irons, convey you to the tower and report back to my commander. All the other officers refused the charge, being much afeared of your majesty, and so it fell to me as I am the lowest rank of any in my regiment. Forgive me, your majesty.

ANNE: Oh excellent! The queen is taken from her palace to a prison by an incompetent lackey, on no one's orders, for no reason.

OFFICER: As you wish, your majesty.

ANNE: And if I should refuse?

OFFICER: If you will not come willingly, I shall be forced to use force.

ANNE: Fool?

FOOL: It appears I have been replaced. You have a new fool now. Farewell, your majesty.

ANNE: You must stay with me.

FOOL: Your majesty—

ANNE: Come with me to the tower.

FOOL: Will you order your faithful Fool to prison?

ANNE: I should not need if you were faithful. Oh, come with me, fool, and laugh with me, fool: my imprisonment is pure folly. Where could a fool be more necessary?

FOOL: Well, then. As I am a Fool…I shall accompany you to chapel.

ANNE: To prison, Fool.

FOOL: More honest prayers have been uttered in that place than in all the great churches of Rome.

OFFICER: Amen.

FOOL: Onward, little man: to freedom! Liberate us from society. Free us from our daily lives—

OFFICER: As you say. This way please.

(l to r): Nancy Drake (Fool), Marina Stephenson Kerr (Anne) and Steve Ratzlaff (Lord Kingston)

## Scene 3: Anne's Chamber in the Tower

*KINGSTON is inspecting the room, ensuring it has been adequately appointed for a queen. LADY KINGSTON bellows from without.*

LADY KINGSTON: (Off.) Husband!

KINGSTON: Here, madam, just finishing up with the—

*LADY KINGSTON enters.*

LADY KINGSTON: The queen is on her way.

KINGSTON: Yes, I know, I was—

LADY KINGSTON: Is everything—

KINGSTON: Yes, yes, I think so.

LADY KINGSTON: And when can we expect Lady Shelton?

KINGSTON: Lady Shelton?

LADY KINGSTON: The king requires another attendant for the duration of the queen's—

KINGSTON: You said that you would speak to—

LADY KINGSTON: You said that you would—

KINGSTON: No I did not. You were to see her on Wednesday last at—

LADY KINGSTON: She wasn't there.

KINGSTON: You might have told me.

LADY KINGSTON: I most distinctly did.

KINGSTON: You did not. Nor do I recall agreeing to contact her—

LADY KINGSTON: Well, you did.

KINGSTON: No, I didn't.

LADY KINGSTON: Yes, you did!

KINGSTON: No, I did not!

***Addle Pated Fool***

LADY KINGSTON: Oh you addle pated fool, I've had my fill of your forgetfulness,
Incompetence and sloppiness and bloody downright laziness,
You never never do what I say!

KINGSTON: I beg your pardon.

LADY KINGSTON: You always have to do it your way.

KINGSTON: Well can you blame—

LADY KINGSTON: You'd think a woman of my breeding, of my parentage and heritage
Would never have consented to so humbling a marriage,
But for fifteen years I've been your wife.

KINGSTON: It feels like fifty.

LADY KINGSTON: You've taken the best years of my life.

KINGSTON: Those were the best?

LADY KINGSTON: And now, in the hour of my triumph,
With the taste of vict'ry sharp upon my tongue;
When I should be as giddy as a maid on her wedding day,
By your incompetence am I undone.

*Music continues under dialogue.*

KINGSTON: I beg to differ.

LADY KINGSTON: Beg all you want, it makes no difference. The queen is coming and we are unprovided. Where, at this late hour, shall we find another lady to attend her? What gentlewoman would be willing to abandon her duties elsewhere? If we must find a Lady of the nobility…

KINGSTON: Must she be a gentlewoman? Surely one of the yeomen's wives would be willing.

LADY KINGSTON: Why need she be a yeoman's wife? Would not any female personage suffice?

KINGSTON: Provided she were suitable to attend upon a queen—

LADY KINGSTON: The queen is a prisoner, and one of the worst kind. One who has demeaned herself in most unnatural ways. Fear not, sir. I shall see that she's accommodated according to her dignity.

KINGSTON: What are you planning, madam?

LADY KINGSTON: *(Singing.)* I knew our situation could be saved by my conniving,
By my scheming and my plotting and my cunning and contriving.

KINGSTON: I must insist you tell me what you'll do.

LADY KINGSTON: Why.

KINGSTON: I cannot leave such business up to you.

LADY KINGSTON: Don't you trust me?
I know a certain woman who would serve the queen discreetly,
Who has seen man's inhumanity yet still speaks sweetly;
The woman who assists the dungeon master;

KINGSTON: You've gone mad.

LADY KINGSTON: She's a perfect—

KINGSTON: —She's an absolute disaster!

LADY KINGSTON: She'll do.
And now, approach the hour of my triumph.
The taste of vict'ry sharp upon my tongue.
I feel about as giddy as a maid on her wedding day.
I shall crow to the world "I've won!"

*Music continues under dialogue.*

KINGSTON: Not so fast not so fast. This, this this this—

LADY KINGSTON: Mistress Stoner?

KINGSTON: She's utterly unsuitable, I must insist—

LADY KINGSTON: *(Looking out the window.)* I do believe that is the queen's barge, is it not, my lord? Just arriving now through the traitors' gate.

*KINGSTON looks out the window. LADY KINGSTON watches him.*

LADY KINGSTON: What do you suggest we do, my lord? I've already arranged it with Stoner; she can be here in a twinkling.

KINGSTON: Make haste.

*LADY KINGSTON exits.*

*(Singing.)* Oh you addle pated fool why do you let her get away with it;
Outfoxed at every turn and simply dandled like an idiot.
She planned this from the very start.
(Just to spite me.)
She likes to think she's so bloody smart.
Well now, in the hour of her triumph,
With the taste of vict'ry sharp upon her tongue,
When she feels as giddy as a maid on her wedding day,
What I wouldn't give to see her undone.

*ANNE enters, followed by the FOOL.*

FOOL: *(Begins off stage.)* Dear God I pray, if you must imprison my body in this tower, imprison also my soul within my flesh.

ANNE: Peace, Fool.

FOOL: Amen.

KINGSTON: Welcome, your royal majesty, to the Tower.

ANNE: Lord Kingston.

KINGSTON: You've brought your fool with you. Not a problem, not a problem—

ANNE: Why am I arrested?

*LADY KINGSTON arrives with MISTRESS STONER.*

KINGSTON: Ah, yes, here we are. Ladies, come and greet the queen.

MISTRESS STONER: Oh my heavens.

KINGSTON: You know my wife, Lady Kingston—

LADY KINGSTON: Welcome.

KINGSTON: And allow me to introduce Mistress Stoner.

MISTRESS STONER: *(Fawning.)* Such an honour to meet you, your majesty! A pleasure, truly! I'm simply—-

LADY KINGSTON: Thank you, that's enough.

MISTRESS STONER: Sorry.

KINGSTON: Yes, thank you.

LADY KINGSTON: I shall attend you here, assisted by Mistress Stoner.

ANNE: That won't be necessary. Send to the palace for the ladies of mine own chamber. They shall serve me.

KINGSTON: I regret that that's not—

LADY KINGSTON: The king has expressly demanded that we be your only attendants.

ANNE: I think it much unkindness of the king to keep from me those who love me.

LADY KINGSTON: We do not question the king's wisdom.

ANNE: Bring me Elizabeth.

KINGSTON: You are denied access to the princess.

ANNE: She is my child.

LADY KINGSTON: In his wisdom, the king has declared—

ANNE: I must speak to him.

KINGSTON: I'm afraid that, too, is denied.

LADY KINGSTON: You are not to address him in word neither spoken nor written.

ANNE: God in heaven, what sort of monster does he take me for?

KINGSTON: Indeed, madam, that brings us to our next point of business. I have here a list of the crimes of which you are accused. I must read them to you, if you please.

ANNE: I would gladly hear them.

FOOL: Fools rush in…

KINGSTON: Very good. Then I shall…read them.

*He clears his throat and reads with great difficulty.*

"Whereas her majesty despising her marriage and entertaining malice against the King and following daily her frail and carnal, um, lust, did falsely and traitorously procure divers of the King's servants to be her adulterers and concubines, and yield to her vile provocations. She procured, by sweet words, kisses, touches and…oh my…

*LORD KINGSTON is quite unable to continue. LADY KINGSTON seizes the opportunity and the paper from him.*

LADY KINGSTON: —by sweet words, kisses, touches and…otherwise, Henry Norris of Westminster, gentleman of the privy chamber, to violate her.

ANNE: God in Heaven.

LADY KINGSTON: Also the Queen procured one William Brerton to violate her at Hampton Court.

ANNE: Rubbish.

LADY KINGSTON: Also the Queen procured Sir Frances Weston of Westminster. Also the Queen procured Mark Smeaton—

ANNE: Smeaton?

LADY KINGSTON: —musician of the privy chamber to violate her at Westminster. Also the Queen—

ANNE: There are others?

LADY KINGSTON: Also the Queen procured and incited her own natural brother George Boleyn to violate her—

MISTRESS STONER: Oh my!

LADY KINGSTON: —alluring him with her tongue in the said George's mouth and the said George's tongue in hers, whereby he, despising the commands of God and all human laws violated and carnally knew the said Queen, his own sister.

FOOL: Unbelievable.

ANNE: You slander the king my husband with these accusations.

LADY KINGSTON: The king himself has signed the charges.

ANNE: They are lies.

LADY KINGSTON: The peers of the court will judge that.

ANNE: Lord Kingston, shall I be denied justice?

KINGSTON: Every subject the king has hath justice.

ANNE: Oh Fool, I am undone.

LADY KINGSTON: Your own evils have been your undoing.

FOOL: Can there be a greater evil than willful ignorance?

LADY KINGSTON: Remember your place.

FOOL: Or is it merely obstinate stupidity? Behold, the coupling of the obstinate ass and the stupid ape renders an asp, who crawls on her belly yet brings queens low.

LADY KINGSTON: Mind how you speak to me, Fool.

FOOL: Heavens yes, I fear you might have me thrown in the Tower.

LADY KINGSTON: Impudent strumpet!

*LADY KINGSTON slaps the FOOL across the face.*

KINGSTON: Madam!

MISTRESS STONER: Oh my goodness me, no!

FOOL: The serpent strikes.

ANNE: Stop it!

LADY KINGSTON: Stop what? *(She slaps the FOOL again.)* Hah?

ANNE: You fiend!

MISTRESS STONER: Turn your face away, madam.

KINGSTON: Lady Kingston.

LADY KINGSTON: My lord?

KINGSTON: Stop your hand! Do you not think the King will take it amiss to see his lady's servant abused by you?

LADY KINGSTON: Do you not think the King will take it amiss to see his lady's servant entertained by you against his express commands? If the slave dislikes my hospitality she is free to seek employment elsewhere.

ANNE: The fool stays.

LADY KINGSTON: Then by this hand she will learn respect for her betters. *(She slaps the FOOL again.)*

ANNE: Enough! Can you not control your wife, sir.

LADY KINGSTON: Thus asks the adulteress.

ANNE: May you have occasion to regret this boldness.

LADY KINGSTON: That shall never be.

ANNE: Lord Kingston, I require some protection for my fool. I will not have her abused by inferior persons.

LADY KINGSTON: I am Lady of this Tower and will maintain order here as I see fit.

ANNE: I am the queen—

LADY KINGSTON: You are the prisoner and under my command.

FOOL: Lord Kingston, I require some protection for my Lady the Queen. I will not have her commanded by inferior—

LADY KINGSTON: Teach that mongrel to heel or I shall beat her into submission.

*LADY KINGSTON viciously strikes the FOOL.*

KINGSTON: Stop it this instant!

LADY KINGSTON: If she stays she will submit to me.

ANNE: Fool, return to court. I have no further need of your services.

FOOL: That is a lie, madam. To take action on a pretense is evil. I cannot be so willfully ignorant, and so I must stay.

LADY KINGSTON: Husband, send the fool away.

KINGSTON: Upon your orders, madam?

LADY KINGSTON: The king's orders—

KINGSTON: The king stated that her ladies were not to be retained, however he has issued no judgments whatever about her fool.

LADY KINGSTON: His will is plain.

KINGSTON: Not to my mind. If the queen requires the fool's presence, we must permit it until a higher authority contradicts the queen's request. We are not to render judgments upon our prisoners. Rather we must accommodate them according to the dignity of their states and carry out the King's commands. I trust you can manage that, woman.

LADY KINGSTON: I can manage very well.

KINGSTON: I cannot keep watch over you, madam. I have many other concerns demanding my attention.

LADY KINGSTON: Oh yes, all those men apprehended with our queen.

ANNE: Who?

LADY KINGSTON: Lords Norris, Brerton, Weston, Mark Smeaton and your brother.

ANNE: They are arrested?

KINGSTON: I'm afraid so.

ANNE: They are also charged…

KINGSTON: With—

LADY KINGSTON: With treason, yes.

ANNE: And they're here?

LADY KINGSTON: Yes.

KINGSTON: Here in—

LADY KINGSTON: In the tower. Such a shame.

ANNE: God have mercy on them.

LADY KINGSTON: Off you go, my lord. You have so much to do, tending to all those men.

KINGSTON: I shall return presently.

ANNE: Yes, thank you.

*KINGSTON exits.*

LADY KINGSTON: But I shouldn't wonder how one man can tend to so many men, when clearly one woman could. You would be well advised to confess.

ANNE: I'll not confess an untruth.

LADY KINGSTON: Confirm what the king already holds to be true. Rest assured confessions will be obtained. The Dungeon Master is very skilled at ferreting out "truth".

FOOL: That is not truth.

MISTRESS STONER: Oh Lady! Oh oh Lady, you must confess! Let not those lovely lads be—

ANNE: Your threats are empty. The men will not be tortured, they are gentlemen.

MISTRESS STONER: Not the one.

FOOL: Smeaton?

MISTRESS STONER: The musician.

FOOL: Poor simple Smeaton.

LADY KINGSTON: He's common, like you two. And he will be constrained to sing.

FOOL: But in an unpleasing tenor.

MISTRESS STONER: He will confess.

FOOL: And how will you sing counterpoint when his false notes are unmannerly stretched to discord?

ANNE: Will none take my part?

LADY KINGSTON: Only a fool, desirous of an early grave.

ANNE: Fool.

FOOL: Madam?

ANNE: Plead for me.

FOOL: To whom, the drunkards in the pub?

ANNE: The king.

LADY KINGSTON: Where are your powerful allies now?

FOOL: I haven't his ear.

ANNE: You have liberty.

FOOL: What use is that?

ANNE: Make him hear you!

LADY KINGSTON: Sending a half-wit mongrel on a knight's errand.

FOOL: From without his chamber door? I'll not be admitted.

ANNE: Use your wit.

FOOL: My wit tells me this is witless.

ANNE: You must find a way: I have no one else.

LADY KINGSTON: England deserves better than a queen whose only ally is a fool.

FOOL: Madam, I would do anything for you.

LADY KINGSTON: Only a fool—

ANNE: Then go.

*The FOOL makes for the door.*

LADY KINGSTON: If you seek the king, he'll not be found at court. He's gone a-courting.

ANNE: Where?

LADY KINGSTON: Hm hm hm…

ANNE: *(To the FOOL.)* Seek him out.

LADY KINGSTON: He's calling on Jane Seymour, England's future queen.

ANNE: That insipid puppet shall never—

LADY KINGSTON: She's younger than you, far prettier, and if she has an opinion of her own in her head, she knows enough to keep it to herself.

FOOL: A paragon of feminine virtue.

ANNE: Who whores herself to the king.

LADY KINGSTON: My niece is a virtuous maid.

FOOL: Jane Seymour is your niece.

LADY KINGSTON: She has the king so wound up that he spins like a child's top; each turn bringing you closer to your death.

ANNE: You lie.

LADY KINGSTON: Send your fool to find out. My niece has many allies in the king's confidence, do you think your pitiful fool can sway him?

ANNE: There are others who hold me dear.

LADY KINGSTON: Yes, clearly, however they too are imprisoned with you.

ANNE: The Archbishop of Canterbury, Thomas Cranmer is much beholden to me. Fool, go speak to him, the king holds him in high esteem and may be swayed in my favour by so virtuous a man of God.

FOOL: I will speak to him, and others if I can.

ANNE: Yes! Thomas Wyatt would sue for me. He loves me well! Here, take this ring to him, tell him of my trials and urge him to speak to the king. But go first to Cranmer.

FOOL: Yes, madam.

ANNE: Oh, Fool, make haste!

FOOL: Fear not, madam.

*The FOOL approaches the door, but LADY KINGSTON blocks her way and holds out her hand.*

LADY KINGSTON: Give it. *(The FOOL refuses.)* How indiscreet. Dispatching love tokens to the one remaining stallion in your filthy stable. Did you think I would overlook such a golden confirmation of your guilt?

*KINGSTON enters.*

My lord, I am sick at heart at what I have to report to you!

KINGSTON: What is amiss?

LADY KINGSTON: The queen even now was attempting to arrange an assignation—

ANNE: That is a lie.

LADY KINGSTON: You cannot deny saying that Thomas Wyatt would sue for you.

ANNE: —that he would speak to the king—

LADY KINGSTON: Is not "one who sues" a suitor?

ANNE: —merely to be my advocate—

LADY KINGSTON: You said he loves you well.

ANNE: In the accepted manner—

LADY KINGSTON: This fool, my lord, was about to be dispatched to one Thomas Wyatt with messages of love and the queen's ring.

KINGSTON: Is this true?

ANNE: No.

KINGSTON: Fool, give me the ring.

FOOL: Ring?

LADY KINGSTON: Fool!

FOOL: It's not mine to give. *(She hands the ring back to ANNE.)*

LADY KINGSTON: See, see!

ANNE: My lord, I am denied all access to my husband the king—

LADY KINGSTON: That justifies an incontinent lust?

ANNE: I must have—

LADY KINGSTON: You need some other man to service you?

ANNE: I will not be insulted—

LADY KINGSTON: You insult the nation with your—

KINGSTON: Enough! *(To MISTRESS STONER.)* Are these accusations true?

MISTRESS STONER: That's not for me to say.

KINGSTON: Was the queen sending a ring to Thomas Wyatt?

MISTRESS STONER: Yes, sir.

KINGSTON: Did she speak of love?

MISTRESS STONER: I'm afraid so, sir.

KINGSTON: I must report this to the king.

LADY KINGSTON: Ha! A confession.

KINGSTON: Well done, Lady Kingston, very well done. Would you be so kind as to prepare my writing desk with paper and ink that I may quickly dispatch this news?

LADY KINGSTON: With pleasure.

*LADY KINGSTON exits.*

ANNE: Please, my lord, my intent was not—

KINGSTON: It is not my place to surmise your intentions, merely to report your words and actions.

ANNE: But I—

KINGSTON: If you give me words, I will faithfully report them to the king.

ANNE: Yes. Lord Kingston, report this:

*Report This*

Like the flower who turns her face only to the sun,
Like the river that flows faithfully to the sea,
Like the solid and unshakable earth beneath your feet,
Am I guilty of inconstancy.
As the rose always grows upon the yew tree,
As the tree's roots ever reach for heaven,
As God's truth burns eternally in the fires of hell,
Has my body been loved by any other men.

Oh tell me wherein I've offended your grace?
What I've done or failed to do?
By God in heaven above me I swear,
My love to you is true.

Though the crops in the fields may be thwarted
By too much or not enough rain,
And autumn's harvest all is disappointment,
Yet still the spring will bloom again!
Oh, say not the land is barren,
Though neglect turns the good soil to mire,
It wants only loving husbandry
To yield unto you your heart's desire.

Oh tell me wherein I've offended your grace?
What I've done or failed to do?
By God in heaven above me I swear,
My love to you is true.

As I have been faithful, have faith in me.
As I have been faithful, have faith in me.
As I have been faithful, have faith in me.
I beg you, I beg you, I beg you, I beg you,
I beg you upon my knees.

KINGSTON: God forgive us.

*LADY KINGSTON enters.*

LADY KINGSTON: Your writing desk was already prepared.

KINGSTON: Was it?

LADY KINGSTON: Yes?

KINGSTON: Oh.

*He begins to leave.*

FOOL: Begging your pardon, sir, but my lady has not been afforded opportunity to pray. Might you seek the King's permission to have Archbishop Thomas Cranmer come to the prison to lead the queen in prayer?

LADY KINGSTON: Oh no.

KINGSTON: A most becoming request.

LADY KINGSTON: You juggler. My lord, do you not perceive—

ANNE: I must make confession.

LADY KINGSTON: My lord, the queen was conspiring to get Cranmer—

KINGSTON: Would you stand between a penitent and her salvation?

LADY KINGSTON: Penitent? She is nothing of the kind.

KINGSTON: To deny her the means of redemption is to deliver her soul to Satan. Are you in league with the devil madam?

FOOL: You need to ask?

LADY KINGSTON: Very well.

KINGSTON: I must go write my report.

LADY KINGSTON: And I will deliver it to the king along with the musician's confession.

KINGSTON: He's confessed?

LADY KINGSTON: He shall. I ordered the dungeon master to interrogate him.

KINGSTON: When?

LADY KINGSTON: Now, when I found your ink and paper at the ready. He's been instructed to pursue the truth with his greatest vigour.

KINGSTON: You have no authority—

LADY KINGSTON: The king wants a confession and I intend to get him one.

ANNE: Lord Kingston—

KINGSTON: Fear not madam, I shall see to this—

LADY KINGSTON: Husband, don't make me report your sympathies for the traitress to the king. He trusts me as one of his closest advisors.

ANNE: I beg you!

LADY KINGSTON: It's probably too late already, I dare say that lovesick troubadour won't last.

ANNE: Please!

KINGSTON: I must…go write my report. By your leave, your majesty.

*KINGSTON exits.*

LADY KINGSTON: *(Calling after him.)* Be sure to make mention of the Fool's unwelcome presence! *(To MISTRESS STONER.)* Get to your post. You're needed in the dungeon.

MISTRESS STONER: Yes, ma'am.

LADY KINGSTON: You'll soon have quite a mess on your hands.

MISTRESS STONER: Bless my soul, there'll be laundry.

*MISTRESS STONER exits, leaving ANNE and LADY KINGSTON alone.*

LADY KINGSTON: Fancy a cup of tea?

## Scene 4: Smeaton's Cell

*MISTRESS STONER and MARK SMEATON enter. His hands are wrapped in bloodied rags. MISTRESS STONER supports his weight as they walk.*

SMEATON: I didn't want to—

MISTRESS STONER: I know, love, I know. Almost there, now.

SMEATON: Will you tell her?

MISTRESS STONER: Of course, love. Lie here, now. You're stronger than you think, you see?

SMEATON: I never wanted to say— She's going to think I— I'm sorry, I'm so so sorry.

MISTRESS STONER: Sh sh sh. Come have a lie down, my sweet. *(She helps him onto his bed.)* There we go. You were very brave.

*(He begins to weep.)* Oh, now not to worry, love, not to worry. 'Twas wisely done; said what he needed to hear. Got it over and done with. *(SMEATON protests.)* There was naught you could do, love, but suffer and lie. And you did both bravely, and with all your heart. Here, take a drop of comfort. *(She sits on the bed and cradles his head like a baby as she tips the bottle to his lips.)* That's it. Let it take you away. Such lovely eyes you have. Oh and lips like the petals of a rose. Come, a bit more, to ease your heart, precious one. My lovely boy-o. Sleep now, it was all just a dream.

(l to r): James Johnston (Mark Smeaton) and Melanie Whyte (Mistress Stoner)

### *Hush Now*

MISTRESS STONER: Hush now, my pretty one, it's over.
Lay your burden down.
Your worried head rest upon my soft breast.
Soon you'll be safe in the ground.
And the flowers will grow
So the whole world will know
That you did your best to be brave and strong.
From the moment of your birth,
'Til you're cradled in the earth,
All we can do is hold on.

Hold on to me let me love you,
Though I'm not the one you adore.
Sweet angels are gathering above you
To welcome a heart so pure.
And the flowers will grow
So the whole world will know
That you did your best to be brave and strong.
From the moment of your birth,
'Til you're cradled in the earth,
All we can do is hold on.

*MISTRESS STONER curls up beside SMEATON and hums gently as the lights fade.*

## Scene 5: The Chapel

*JANE SEYMOUR is alone, pretending to pray. LADY KINGSTON enters and kneels beside her.*

LADY KINGSTON: Good news, Mistress Seymour.

JANE SEYMOUR: *(Startled.)* Lady Kingston!

LADY KINGSTON: Not who you expected?

JANE SEYMOUR: I'm waiting for the king.

LADY KINGSTON: I know. Your secret little assignation's the talk of the court.

JANE SEYMOUR: But I've not breathed a word—

LADY KINGSTON: The future queen's activities are of great interest to everyone.

JANE SEYMOUR: Will I be queen?

LADY KINGSTON: I have a confession right here from one of the old queen's consorts.

JANE SEYMOUR: So he can kill her?

LADY KINGSTON: With a clear conscience.

JANE SEYMOUR: God be praised! And may her soul find peace in heaven.

LADY KINGSTON: Now you mustn't let your great ambition get the better of your judgment.

JANE SEYMOUR: No?

LADY KINGSTON: No.

### *Kill the Brat*

LADY KINGSTON: Though the queen will be dead, I still perceive an impediment,
That might thwart your success therefore, I believe it expedient
To eliminate any and all potential threats.
And by threats I mean that brat the princess Elizabeth.

Kill the brat I say,
To clear the way
For your own child to take the crown.
She's an ugly thing,
What good could it bring,
To let her stick around?
The queen's an adulterous whore.
That the king is the father we will never be sure.
Though you might fear you're being unkind,
Kill the brat for your own peace of mind.

JANE SEYMOUR: But the king loves his daughter.

LADY KINGSTON: Alas, 'tis true.

JANE SEYMOUR: And we can't kill the princess
So what shall we do?

LADY KINGSTON: If the king loves the child then we must proceed by degrees.
Like a cancer cultivate discontent's disease.
If the king would annul his matrimonial knot;
The marriage dissolved, a princess she is not!

Kill the brat I say,
To clear the way
For your own child to take the crown.
She's an ugly thing
What good could it bring
To let her stick around?
The queen's an adulterous whore.

JANE SEYMOUR: Is the king the father?

LADY KINGSTON: We'll never be sure.

BOTH: Though you/I might fear you're/I'm being unkind
Kill the brat for your/my own peace of mind.

JANE SEYMOUR: Annul the marriage?

LADY KINGSTON: Now you get it!

JANE SEYMOUR: That will be easy,
He deeply regrets it!

TOGETHER: Once the child is a bastard her secret execution
Will easily be brought to its conclusion.
Just picture the wee thing hoisted on a spear!
Or strangled or poisoned it makes me have to cheer:

LADY KINGSTON: Kill the brat I say!
Kill the brat I say!

(l to r): Cory Wojcik (Henry VIII) and Miriam Smith (Lady Kingston)

JANE SEYMOUR: Kill the brat?

TOGETHER: Kill the brat,
Kill the brat,
Kill the brat—

*HENRY enters and the music abruptly shifts to gentle innocuous strains.*

HENRY: Good even, Mistress Seymour.

JANE SEYMOUR: Your highness.

HENRY: Lady Kingston, what a surprise.

LADY KINGSTON: Your Royal Highness. I must deliver these letters to you, one from my husband concerning diverse requests from the queen, and a document from Master Smeaton. The musician was persuaded to sing.

HENRY: I thank you. *(He tucks the letters away and looks at LADY KINGSTON, waiting for her to leave.)*

LADY KINGSTON: But now I must return to my charge. By your leave.

HENRY: Most certainly.

LADY KINGSTON: Fare you well, your highness. Mistress?

*LADY KINGSTON and JANE join hands to say farewell.*

TOGETHER: *(Singing.)* Kill the brat!

*LADY KINGSTON exits.*

HENRY: Come hither, my sweet, and let me kiss your lips.

JANE SEYMOUR: Forgive a poor subject who disobeys her lord, but I fear my honour may be beggared by my obedience.

HENRY: You prize honour over obedience?

JANE SEYMOUR: Indeed, for honour is bred in the bone, while obedience equivocates according to her will.

HENRY: Obedience to her King will never tarnish a maid's honour.

JANE SEYMOUR: Until she births a bastard.

HENRY: Your sons will not be bastards, lady, but princes. I want you to be my queen.

JANE SEYMOUR: Oh my sweet sweet lord! But how can that be? She who wears the crown still lives, her every breath a torment to your grace.

HENRY: She shall not live for long.

JANE SEYMOUR: I thank your grace. And yet, if I am to be queen…

HENRY: You shall be queen.

JANE SEYMOUR: Shall I be expected to wear a secondhand crown?

HENRY: I shall make you a dozen rich crowns to grace your pretty brow.

JANE SEYMOUR: But my title should be handed down to me from a woman of…questionable honour. I should be known as a whore's substitute.

HENRY: I defy anyone who dares accuse you thus.

JANE SEYMOUR: But it will be said. Furthermore, I would not have our true and lawful heirs threatened by that witch's spawn.

HENRY: What are you demanding?

JANE SEYMOUR: Untie the knot you knit under the influence of witchcraft. Annul your marriage to the so-called queen.

HENRY: But she will die.

JANE SEYMOUR: The mother's death is not enough if the ill-gotten child remains a princess. Forgive my boldness, born of my anguish at seeing you so abused. Oh break my heart!

HENRY: Hush, hush my sweet. All things shall be as you desire. If my divorcing the queen will give you peace—

JANE SEYMOUR: It shall, it shall!

HENRY: How could I deny you anything? Come, let me kiss your tears away.

JANE SEYMOUR: You are too good. Forgive my forward tongue, my prating lips.

HENRY: Oh, let me teach them both a better service.

JANE SEYMOUR: In time, my dearest love, for now be chaste, lest the giving rend the gift diminished.

HENRY: I'll speed the time. *(Calling.)* Sirrah! I'll whip old man time into a jig and in a twinkling you'll be queen.

*Enter SIRRAH.*

SIRRAH: My Lord?

HENRY: Summon Archbishop Cranmer in here. Make haste, I would speak with him presently.

SIRRAH: I shall my Lord.

*He exits.*

JANE SEYMOUR: What will you do?

HENRY: What can I not do? I am King. Yet I wish only to humble myself to be your servant, to kneel at your feet and satisfy your deepest longing.

JANE SEYMOUR: And your service shall be paid and double paid, and all the pains you suffer now will serve to sweeten the pleasure of the payment.

*Enter CRANMER.*

CRANMER: God's praise be with your majesty.

HENRY: My noble Archbishop, welcome, I thank you for your haste. Leave me, madam, I shall anon to your chamber to give report of this interview and to receive such thanks as you see meet to give.

JANE SEYMOUR: But you shall owe me favours for inflicting upon me the tediousness of your absence. Were I ignorant of the cause, I fear I should languish from the effort. My Lord, adieu.

*JANE exits.*

CRANMER: I humbly thank you for granting me audience today. These suspicions I hear about the queen are most distressing to me.

HENRY: And to me! I cannot eat, I cannot sleep without that horrid word "cuckold" laughing at my injuries.

CRANMER: My lord, you have been abused.

HENRY: Indeed.

CRANMER: Then give me leave to assure you, these charges against the queen are patently false. She is not a traitor and you are not a cuckold.

HENRY: What are you saying? I put my own hand to her arrest warrant. Did I do so in error?

CRANMER: You may have been misled, for I had never better opinion of woman.

HENRY: But if the peers of the court should find her guilty—

CRANMER: I understand. I shall speak to the men of your council urging them to find her innocent.

HENRY: They are of a mind to convict her.

CRANMER: If I should acquaint them, in the roundest terms, of your Grace's pleasure, who among them would dare defy his King?

HENRY: What are you suggesting? That my will should determine the verdict of this trial?

CRANMER: No, my lord.

HENRY: I seek only the truth in this matter.

CRANMER: The truth, your grace, is that the queen has been slandered, I am sure of it. I have known her since she was a child—

HENRY: You are a fool: you know her not at all. Here, unseal this.

*(HENRY hands CRANMER the confession.)* You needn't take my word for it, read it for yourself. She may have been virtuous as a child, but that child is dead. It was becoming queen that changed her. When one is born into royalty one learns from an early age to temper power's corrupting influence. But she—oh she is corrupt.

CRANMER: My lord.

HENRY: You see now, you see what she is.

CRANMER: This confession—

HENRY: Yes, I know! It is never easy to sound the depth of depravity in one who held your trust.

CRANMER: But this confession was clearly given under duress. There's blood upon the page. See here—

HENRY: Do not wag that thing in my face. Would you force me to look on my shame? I do not care to know the particulars: it is a confession, it will suffice.

CRANMER: Yet I fear you are being misled.

HENRY: Why do you defend her?

CRANMER: I love her well and I—

HENRY: Oh Thomas!

CRANMER: Your grace—

HENRY: You vile, dissembling monster!

CRANMER: My lord?

HENRY: Have you lain with my wife?

CRANMER: I swear before God, I have not!

HENRY: Liar!

CRANMER: My lord, I beg you—

HENRY: She was enjoyed by her own brother, why not by you?

CRANMER: Could I stand before you and declare my love for the queen if I held in my heart any trace of sin? Would I seek out your favour to plead in her defense? Or would I rather avoid your grace, hide me in my house and sigh in relief that she who knew my sin would soon be safely in her grave?

HENRY: Oh I am surrounded by scorpions, I can trust no one.

CRANMER: May God forgive me if aught that I have done has given you reason to distrust me.

HENRY: Do you believe this testimony is truth?

CRANMER: Only God can know the truth. But I humbly pledge my obedience to your grace's will.

HENRY: It is my will that you should believe it.

CRANMER: Then I shall labour to honour your will.

HENRY: Labour to save my honour. I shall not be mocked as a cuckold.

CRANMER: Her crime is to her dishonour, my lord, not your own.

HENRY: As husband to a harlot I am dishonoured. You must spare me that fate.

CRANMER: Your grace?

HENRY: Our marriage should never have happened. That woman was never my wife, not in the all-seeing eyes of God. You erred when you bound us together, correct that error now by breaking the bonds. Annul my marriage.

CRANMER: But that would make Elizabeth—

HENRY: She is a bastard, tainted with her mother's blood. I am sick when I look on her.

CRANMER: I understand your Grace's will—

HENRY: My will? This is God's will!

CRANMER: I must have grounds. If your marriage should not have taken place. There must have been preexisting conditions which—

HENRY: There were indeed: she will need to make a final confession before her death, and I have no doubt that her confession will furnish you with adequate grounds for annulment.

CRANMER: I shall undertake it, your Highness.

HENRY: I will send word to Kingston that you are to have private access to the Queen, so she will be encouraged to speak freely.

CRANMER: I would welcome the chance to see her, to give your grace the means to ease your troubled soul.

HENRY: I am putting my trust in you, Thomas. Do not make me wonder what might occur behind closed doors between you and that known seductress. I would be loathe to lose your fair presence in court.

CRANMER: I will not fail.

HENRY: Do not. I'll send word to Kingston directly. Fare you well.

CRANMER: May God be with you.

*CRANMER exits.*

HENRY: Sirrah!

SIRRAH: *(Entering.)* Yes, my Lord?

HENRY: There is an expert swordsman living in Calais, an executioner of exceeding good report. Send for him directly.

SIRRAH: I shall, my Lord. *(Exits.)*

HENRY: Yes.

*Alone, HENRY unfolds the confession and reads it.*

**Scene 6: The Trial**

*ANNE stands isolated in a pool of light down stage centre. The disembodied voice of LORD NORFOLK blares out.*

LORD NORFOLK: Mistress Anne Boleyn, you are hereby charged with treason. These peers of the court have gathered to be your jury. Good. Men. All. Stand forth and be judged.

*The women of the cast join ANNE, each isolated in her own light. They face the audience and sing.*

***The Women's Song***

MEN: A woman stands on trial for sins of the flesh.

WOMEN: Again.

MEN: And who will we blame for her predicament?

WOMEN: The men.

MEN: But is it the men, her sins or society we should blame?
Or is her body the thing that brings her shame?

WOMEN: Like Eve, the mother of us all
Whose cleverness is called "the fall",
We're all judged by what our bodies can or can't achieve
If ever we are reckoned
By intelligence it's second,
Our brains won't be the legacy we leave.

We must have babies, so the species will survive
For we are duty bound to keep mankind alive.
Until we do we're not worth the trouble our bodies cause.
Oh, we are morally weak, though lovely, and tragically flawed.

Like Jezebel, the stinking whore
Who put on lipstick, nothing more,
Woman's judged by how she tries to cover up her skin:
If she covers too much, she's a prude
Not enough, she's cheap and lewd
There's only one way that a girl can win:

We must have babies, so the species will survive
For we are duty bound to keep mankind alive.
Until we do we're not worth the trouble our bodies cause.
Oh, we are morally weak, though lovely, and tragically flawed.

And we are judged, we are judged,
For the power to seduce,
And the urge to reproduce.
We are hated, we're despised,

We are feared and demonized,
We can see within your eyes
Ourselves reflected at our most abhorrent;
Ours sins and failings strike us as a torrent;
Until drenched in our shame we see
The wretches we have come to be.
We're condemned, we are cursed,
Undeserving of man's love,
Anathema to God above.
We are vile, we are shamed,
Our flesh pollutes the earth,
We are redeemed by giving birth.

We must have babies, so the species will survive.
We must justify our right to stay alive.
Until we do we're not worth the trouble our bodies cause.
Oh, we are morally weak, though lovely, and tragically flawed.
Ahhh-ahhh-ahhh-ahhh-ahhh-ahhh-ahh
Ahhh ahhh ahhh ah ah-ahh-ahh-ahh-ahhh

MEN: GUILTY!

*Intermission.*

# Act Two

## Scene 1: Anne's Chamber

*MISTRESS STONER is waiting, LADY KINGSTON enters.*

LADY KINGSTON: Tis concluded, not five minutes since. She'll be here presently.

MISTRESS STONER: But what was the outcome?

LADY KINGSTON: If she was innocent she would be free to go. As she is to return here…

MISTRESS STONER: But her sentence?

LADY KINGSTON: She'll either be burnt or beheaded.

MISTRESS STONER: Oh heavens, no. He wouldn't burn her, would he?

LADY KINGSTON: The King will decide his pleasure.

MISTRESS STONER: But burning: it's so drawn out. So undignified. I couldn't bear to see the lady suffer so.

LADY KINGSTON: Well you may just have to. So make yourself ready.

*KINGSTON leads in ANNE, followed by the FOOL.*

KINGSTON: Ladies.

LADY KINGSTON: Welcome sir, madam.

KINGSTON: The prisoner is a proved traitress and has been sentenced to die the death. She is no longer your Queen, for she has been stripped of her titles. But with the aid of charitable friends, she may repent her wickedness and enjoy the glory of God's benevolence in the hereafter. Therefore I insist that you accommodate her with charity.

LADY KINGSTON: We will, sir.

FOOL: Save your efforts. The prisoner deserves no charity.

KINGSTON: Come come, Fool.

FOOL: She deserves justice. Where there is justice there is no need for charity.

KINGSTON: Now, Fool, I caution you—

FOOL: But in this kingdom we make a prisoner grovel for your scraps of charity when we should behold a queen feasting on justice.

LADY KINGSTON: We shall soon see a Fool reap her just rewards for insolence.

MISTRESS STONER: Could I offer her majesty some comfort, Sir?

LADY KINGSTON: She is not your majesty.

ANNE: Would I had never seen the day.

MISTRESS STONER: Take a wee dram, madam.

FOOL: A dram for my damned dam.

MISTRESS STONER: 'Tisn't ambrosia, but it does take the edge off.

FOOL: Drink, Lady.

LADY KINGSTON: Drink to your continued good health!

KINGSTON: Lady...

*The FOOL tries to give the flask to ANNE, but she refuses it.*

LADY KINGSTON: To life!

FOOL: I'll drink to that.

ANNE: No. *(Taking the flask from the FOOL.)* To death. And the comfort it brings. *(She drinks.)*

KINGSTON: Indeed. And to that end, I have received word from the King that Archbishop Cranmer is coming to hear your final confession. He shall be here anon.

ANNE: Send him away.

KINGSTON: The king has granted you a private conference with him; thus may you give free reign to your conscience and confess those sins which might otherwise keep you from the heavenly realm.

LADY KINGSTON: 'Twill be quite a litany.

ANNE: I am innocent.

LADY KINGSTON: Hah.

KINGSTON: Nevertheless, he is coming. I am also given to understand that the King has sent for a French executioner from Calais, a swordsman. He arrives within three days.

LADY KINGSTON: Chop chop!

KINGSTON: Come, Lady Kingston, let us go to greet this Bishop.

LADY KINGSTON: Adieu, Mistress Anne.

*He leads LADY KINGSTON to the door and ushers her out ahead of himself.*

ANNE: Jesu protect me.

KINGSTON: *(Sneaking back.)* This swordsman is very skilled, madam, and will offer you a quick and painless death. You needn't fear the scaffold.

LADY KINGSTON: *(Off.)* Lord Kingston!

(l to r): Melanie Whyte (Mistress Stoner) and Nancy Drake (Fool)

KINGSTON: *(Calling.)* By and by. *(To ANNE.)* Take comfort, madam.

*LORD KINGSTON exits.*

FOOL: It is a gentle and benevolent King who would offer his most miserable subject such charity.

MISTRESS STONER: Oh, that swordsman is lovely! I've seen him work, he's exquisite!

FOOL: So I've heard.

MISTRESS STONER: He's the best there is. And handsome? You could do worse than have sight of him as your last look at the world.

FOOL: Why, Mistress Stoner.

MISTRESS STONER: Honestly, Fool, he's gorgeous!

FOOL: Drop dead gorgeous?

MISTRESS STONER: Oh yes!

***The Swordsman of Calais (a tango)***

FOOL: He's got designs on you, that Swordsman of Calais,
You can tell he wants to do it: do it to you today.
You may feel a little wan
At the thought of Acheron,
But surrender and you will be well rewarded.
Look at the gleam in his eye,
Rippling biceps, bulging thigh,
And feel your morbid thoughts give over to the sordid.

MISTRESS STONER: That's what his sword did!
And all the women in the square,
Slack jawed and flustered as they stare.

FOOL: The swordsman seems a sort of deity;
God of mortality.

MISTRESS STONER: How can a heartless assassin
Fill my body with such passion?
How can aversion transform into lust?

FOOL: To what yearning do we yield?
What guilty truth do we reveal?

MISTRESS STONER: Don't question, just
Surrender to it now and trust.

TOGETHER: What a pleasure to be taken by the Swordsman of Calais,
With his shining gleaming length of tempered steel.
No woman would be tempted to go any other way
If her status could contrive her such a deal.
Hanging is undignified, the guillotine's demeaning,
And being drawn and quartered's such a drag.
But your death will be sanctified, your face will still be smiling
As they toss your severed head into the body bag.

FOOL: Flushed with anticipation
Of your decapitation,
You step with confidence sublime,
For the very last time.
Perhaps you'll falter as you go,
Though you're moving very slow,
Weighed down with all your petty earthly woe.
Just make it up the scaffold stair,
You can leave your burden there;
He'll gently sever troubled thoughts from body's care.

TOGETHER: What a pleasure to be taken by the Swordsman of Calais
With his shining gleaming length of tempered steel.
No woman would be tempted to go any other way
If her status could contrive her such a deal.

Hanging is undignified, the guillotine's demeaning,
And being drawn and quartered's such a drag.
But your death will be sanctified, your face will still be smiling
As they toss your severed head into the body bag.

*LADY KINGSTON and CRANMER enter at the end of the song.*

LADY KINGSTON: Presenting the Archbishop of Canterbury, Thomas Cranmer.

CRANMER: Good day.

LADY KINGSTON: Such a prestigious visitor for a commoner like Mistress Anne. Come along Ladies, we must give the prisoner privacy.

*LADY KINGSTON and MISTRESS STONER head for the door, but the FOOL doesn't join them.*

Fool?

ANNE: Stay.

FOOL: I must stay.

LADY KINGSTON: The king demands—

FOOL: The queen demands—

LADY KINGSTON: I see no queen here.

FOOL: The lady cannot unfold her heart to her confessor if her conscience has abandoned her. Ergo, I must remain.

LADY KINGSTON: My husband shall hear of it.

*LADY KINGSTON sweeps from the room, followed reluctantly by MISTRESS STONER. ANNE refuses to look at either of them. There is an awkward pause.*

FOOL: Will you greet your guest, Lady? Or must I take your part? *(To CRANMER.)* Patience, good sir. The queen has had a trying day. She has been tried today. And betrayed today by men who should love her. Her uncle Lord Norfolk, her old love, Lord Percy. Shallow sycophants, there's not a scrap of integrity in the lot: a pack of Judases! *(To ANNE.)* Come, Lady, your friend is here now.

CRANMER: I should not have come. Forgive me—

*He makes for the door, but ANNE stops him with her words.*

ANNE: No! Thomas, stay. Please please stay.

*ANNE takes CRANMER's hand but he recoils slightly.*

CRANMER: Forgive me, your majesty.

ANNE: My dear dear—

CRANMER: No—

ANNE: —dear friend.

CRANMER: Address me not so—

ANNE: Thomas.

CRANMER: Madam?

ANNE: Thomas, I tell you from my soul that they are lies.

CRANMER: I have no doubt of your innocence.

ANNE: Yet you cannot meet my gaze?

CRANMER: I dare not.

ANNE: God in heaven. What is your fear?

CRANMER: Mine own unworthiness.

ANNE: Thomas, I will not hear of it.

CRANMER: I am sent here to betray our friendship, your honour and my integrity. The king has made a demand…

ANNE: What more could he want? I am dead.

CRANMER: Your daughter lives.

ANNE: What have you been sent to do?

CRANMER: I am to annul your marriage.

ANNE: To bastardize my child.

CRANMER: I fear so.

ANNE: Upon what grounds?

CRANMER: That is what I am sent to discover.

ANNE: I am deceived.

CRANMER: Forgive me.

ANNE: No it is you who must forgive me. I can offer you no grounds to annul my marriage.

CRANMER: Very well. *(He makes for the door, but stops himself.)* Anne, my friendship with you is questioned. If I fail to give the king what he wants, I fear the worst.

ANNE: You are suspected of—

CRANMER: Yes.

FOOL: A merrier cuckold was there never: finding new lovers for his wife every hour!

ANNE: How could he be a cuckold? He denies he is my husband!

FOOL: True.

ANNE: That's it! He wants an annulment. I want to live. *(To CRANMER.)* And you want to live. We can all be satisfied: you may annul my marriage, but you must first make the king promise to spare my life.

CRANMER: I fear I would be risking my own life.

ANNE: If I was never his wife I cannot have been unfaithful.

CRANMER: I dare not anger the king.

ANNE: I must sacrifice my child's welfare to protect your life, but you hesitate to make a simple request of the king in order to save mine. Go to the king with empty pockets. Beg his forgiveness that you have failed in his embassy.

FOOL: Madam, consider—

CRANMER: Anne, please—

ANNE: You love me not!

FOOL: You ask too much!

CRANMER: Tell me what you would have me say to the king. I shall bargain for your life for you.

ANNE: God bless you, Thomas, tell him I would live. He needn't keep me: there is a protestant convent in Antwerp, I am friendly with the Abbess there. I shall leave England and live as a nun. And when he is dead I shall return.

FOOL: But what of the child?

ANNE: Elizabeth? She shall remain here.

FOOL: Without the protection of her royal title she would be vulnerable to—

ANNE: If I am to live that is what must be done. She's only a girl, what good is she? She'd never rule England. *(To CRANMER.)* You are her godfather, you will see to her.

CRANMER: Most certainly. And the grounds?

ANNE: To annul my marriage.

CRANMER: Yes.

*Long pause.*

FOOL: You know what he wants.

ANNE: I do not.

FOOL: You saw him today.

ANNE: I did not.

FOOL: Very well.

CRANMER: What?

FOOL: *(Punning relentlessly on PERCY.)* I perceive that there is some personal reason—

ANNE: I have it. His liaison with my sister.

CRANMER: Anne.

ANNE: He flaunted his affair with her in court for more than a year.

CRANMER: She ceased to be his mistress long before you were married.

ANNE: As she is my sister, our marriage was a trespass of the bounds of affinity set out in Leviticus.

CRANMER: It will not suffice.

ANNE: But he clearly loved her.

CRANMER: Love is not enough.

FOOL: The king's love will not suffice, that's certain. He suffers from a tragic lack of manly vigour: he fails to rise to the occasion, to thrust forward into immortality!

ANNE: Enough!

FOOL: Surely a man's refusal to fill his wife's eager belly with sons is grounds for annulment.

CRANMER: If our lady's husband were a man.

FOOL: And not a monster.

CRANMER: Not a king.

FOOL: Ah yes.

CRANMER: Anne, can you conceive of any reason—

ANNE: None.

FOOL: The lady cannot conceive, sir, there's the rub! For if our lady's husband were a man and not a king, she would have sons by now. If our lady's husband were a man and not a king she would not be awaiting execution. If our lady's husband were a man and not a king, she would not be queen, but Lady Percy.

ANNE: Peace, Fool!

FOOL: You know what the king wants to hear.

ANNE: What, lies?

FOOL: You loved Lord Percy.

ANNE: He never loved me.

FOOL: I spoke with him today outside the courtroom—

ANNE: Where he pronounced my guilt.

FOOL: He begs your forgiveness, he had no choice. He told me—

ANNE: Peace, Fool!

FOOL: That he would always love —

ANNE: Quiet! Thomas, please, my sister…

CRANMER: Had you promised yourself to Percy?

FOOL: She had given herself to Percy.

ANNE: Peace, Fool!

CRANMER: Anne, is this true?

ANNE: I will not give him this!

FOOL: It's what he wants.

ANNE: He knows already.

CRANMER: What?

FOOL: They had pledged themselves to one another, but the king denied them permission to be married.

CRANMER: Anne, you swore that you'd never pledged yourself to—

ANNE: I lied! I swore an oath before God and I lied! I perjured myself in order to marry Henry. And Henry knew, yet there we stood before you, wearing masks of piety, vowing ignorance of any impediment to our marriage. I swore against my heart—against God—that I had never promised myself to any man. But I lied, Thomas, I lied before God!

CRANMER: I see.

FOOL: Surely this is what the king sent you here to 'discover'.

ANNE: Congratulations, sir, I expect that confession will win you great favour with the king.

CRANMER: Oh Anne…

### *What Must You Think of Me?*

ANNE: What must you think of me,
Now that you know what I am?
I have betrayed my heart, feigning I've played my part,
Now here I stand,
Condemned at mine own hand.
What must you think of me?

CRANMER: What must you think of me?
I've known you so many years,
Now you fear
I would abandon you,
When I should by mine honour be true?
What must you think of me?

ANNE: I will not look you in the eye—

CRANMER: I am unworthy of your regard.

ANNE: Clothed in tattered remnants of a lie.

CRANMER: How could I be so hard?

BOTH: My shame a show for all the world to see:
What must you think,
What must you think,
What must you think of me?

ANNE: Go! Why do you tarry?
Tell the king all you have heard;
Sure it will make him merry!
Sure it is what I deserve.
What must you think of me,
Now that you know what I am?
I have betrayed my heart, feigning I've played my part,
Now here I stand,
Condemned at mine own hand.
What must you think of me?

CRANMER: I would rather take an infant from his mother
And leave him for the ravens of the heath
Than to profane the sanctity of love's first flower
By bearing it like battle spoils to love's own thief.
The God of Love is of all kingdoms king
And to his laws I adhere obediently,
And in my heart you'll always be the queen.
What must you think of me?
What must you think of me?
I've known you so many years
Now you fear
I would abandon you,
When I should by mine honour be true?
What must you think of me?

ANNE: What will you say?

CRANMER: I shall sue for your life.

ANNE: But of the annulment. He wants my confession of love for Lord Percy.

CRANMER: Yes.

ANNE: What will you say?

CRANMER: Shall I betray you or kill you?

ANNE: Oh, Thomas.

CRANMER: Selfish as I am, I would not let you go.

ANNE: Tell him what you need to say.

CRANMER: Yes…

ANNE: And if my life cannot be saved, I will see you when I make my last confession.

CRANMER: 'Til we meet again.

ANNE: Oh, Thomas, would you do your friend another favour and bear this ring to Lord Percy with my fondest regards?

CRANMER: You saw him collapse in the courtroom. I fear he did not recover his spirit.

ANNE: I see.

CRANMER: I'm sorry.

ANNE: Not at all. This *(She refers to the ring.)* was just a trifling whim. Of no importance. So, he is dead. And I shall be a nun.

CRANMER: I'll do my best to make it so.

ANNE: God's love upon you, Thomas.

CRANMER: And upon you.

*CRANMER exits.*

ANNE: Come, Fool, help me prepare for my journey.

FOOL: To God?

ANNE: To Antwerp.

FOOL: As I said, to God.

*MISTRESS STONER enters, flask at the ready.*

MISTRESS STONER: Oh her Ladyship is in a state! *(She drinks.)* Dear God deliver us!

*LADY KINGSTON enters.*

LADY KINGSTON: Well done, Fool, your insolence has earned you a permanent place here in the Tower. I've arranged to keep you here indefinitely after Mistress Anne's execution.

ANNE: That won't be necessary, Lady Kingston, the Fool will come with me.

LADY KINGSTON: Our former Queen has become the sort of barbarian who takes her servants with her to the grave?

FOOL: Oh yes, the grave! For gravity is the law in a convent.

LADY KINGSTON: A convent?

FOOL: In Antwerp.

LADY KINGSTON: How now, how now? What is this convent?

MISTRESS STONER: I believe our Lady is hoping to sacrifice her life to God, rather than die on the scaffold, isn't that so?

LADY KINGSTON: You're going to be a nun?

ANNE: With the king's approval, yes.

LADY KINGSTON: In Antwerp?

ANNE: I am familiar with the abbess there, yes.

LADY KINGSTON: Hah. I shall have to arrange a sojourn in Antwerp if that is so. Oh, how it would thrill my heart to see you on hands and knees humbly scrubbing the stone step of the abbey. And what of your fancy men? Will our monasteries be flooded with a great wave of new penitents? Or will they die upon the morrow as planned?

ANNE: Tomorrow?

LADY KINGSTON: No hope of reprieve for them.

MISTRESS STONER: A dreadful shame.

LADY KINGSTON: You can listen for the cannons midmorning, one blast will salute the death of each of the traitors. Or perhaps it would please Mistress Anne to watch the executions. Do you fancy an outing up yonder hill?

ANNE: Go to!

LADY KINGSTON: I will certainly be there.

MISTRESS STONER: Am I required to attend as usual?

LADY KINGSTON: Of course. Mistress Stoner loves executions; I've never known her to miss one.

MISTRESS STONER: I am required to be there, to clean up afterwards and—

LADY KINGSTON: Come come, Mistress Stoner, you love to see it.

MISTRESS STONER: Oh no, I don't watch the dying, I turn my face to the wall when the axe drops.

LADY KINGSTON: What a waste.

MISTRESS STONER: But I do truly love to see the men before— just before. That moment when death's certain and there's naught to be done but surrender to it. Summoning the courage to bear the axe…

ANNE: Heaven help me.

MISTRESS STONER: A man is ne'er more beautiful than at that moment, provided he faces it with courage and grace.

ANNE: I see no beauty in the untimely death of my dear brother. Only devastation!

MISTRESS STONER: Forgive me, Lady.

LADY KINGSTON: Certain you'll not join us?

ANNE: Fie!

LADY KINGSTON: Then start praying, nun.

*MISTRESS STONER and LADY KINGSTON exit.*

**Scene 2: The Chapel**

*HENRY and JANE enter.*

JANE SEYMOUR: But there's no one here at all!

HENRY: What? Where is that blasted bishop?

JANE SEYMOUR: You've led me on a merry chase, I now begin to fear I am the quarry, to be seduced within these sacred walls.

HENRY: Not at all, my beloved, the tardy cleric will be here anon.

JANE SEYMOUR: Until he comes, we are alone. I pray you, sir, stand not so close.

HENRY: The nearer to thee, the nearer to heaven, my love. My thoughts of you are holy.

JANE SEYMOUR: Pertaining to a hole?

HENRY: Let me read you scriptures, the Song of Songs, my beloved? Perhaps a psalm about the rod and staff? Let me speak in tongues and fill you with holy rapture.

JANE SEYMOUR: Such delightful suggestions, but I must tell you no.

HENRY: For mercy's sake?

JANE SEYMOUR: No.

HENRY: Can I not tempt you?

JANE SEYMOUR: No.

HENRY: Oh!

*A Girl Who Won't Put Out*

HENRY: The sexiest thing, without a doubt
Is a girl who won't put out.
There's nothing makes a gent want to go
Like that demure but emphatic word NO!
I get quite turned off by demands and insistence,
But the thing I can't resist is resistance,
So girl if you've got your eye on a man;
Do nothing as hard as you can.

JANE SEYMOUR: If you've set your hungry heart on a King,

Don't give in till he gives you a ring.
If he begs you to please go down,
Say "No head until my head is sporting a crown."
I get quite turned off by demands and insistence,
But the thing I can't resist is resistance.
You'll either be branded a whore or a Queen;
There's nothing in between.

HENRY: If a maid gives in too easily,
It makes me feel quite queasily,
That she's betrayed her honour once or twice.
And then I cannot treasure
Thoughts of corporeal pleasure
Without fearing I'll end up covered in lice.
It would be in the very worst taste
To feed a king from another man's plate.
I have no sexual preference for deference;
Just an erotic reliance on defiance.
For a King that's a hell of a thing!
Come over here, Janey, lemme hear you sing!

JANE SEYMOUR: No, no no no no NO!
No, no no no no NO!
No, no no no no no no no no NO!
No, no no no no NO!

HENRY & JANE SEYMOUR: The sexiest thing, without a doubt
Is a girl who won't put out.
There's nothing makes a gent want to go
Like that demure but emphatic word NO!
I get quite turned off by demands and insistence,
But the thing I can't resist is resistance:
So girl if you've got your eye on a man,
Do nothing as hard as you can.

*CRANMER enters and they are caught in flagrante, sort of.*

HENRY: My good bishop, welcome.

CRANMER: My Lord, Lady.

HENRY: You're late. I hope your report will excuse the offense.

CRANMER: It is my deepest wish.

HENRY: Here I have the papers laid out, you need only fill in the particulars here and sign it at the bottom and so ends an unfortunate chapter in my otherwise happy life. And so breaks the dawn of a brighter happiness, my beloved. Here is a pen, here ink, about it man.

CRANMER: My Lord, the lady has put forth a modest and most becoming request, for as you know, this intelligence has cost her child her title. And therefore she appeals to your charity—

HENRY: That I shall honour my obligations as the child's father, yes, yes of course.

CRANMER: Her request is not that, my Lord. She knows your kind and generous nature wouldn't suffer you to deprive your child of anything. Her request concerns not earthly relationships, but rather, her connection to the divine.

HENRY: On with it. Fie how you mumble on.

CRANMER: She begs you, my Lord, to spare her life and let her find sanctuary in Antwerp, to live out her days in holy contemplation at the convent there.

HENRY: Antwerp?

CRANMER: That is her request, my Lord.

HENRY: What, are all the fools of the globe gone to dwell in Antwerp? How else to explain the expectation of a vile whore to be welcomed into a holy sisterhood.

JANE SEYMOUR: In Antwerp!

HENRY: Did you ever hear the like?

JANE SEYMOUR: *(Crossing herself in mock piety.)* Heaven help us.

HENRY: Heaven help Antwerp!

CRANMER: She is genuinely remorseful for having angered you so and asks for this opportunity purely for the chance to serve God. She feels the time left her is inadequate to atone for all her sins.

HENRY: Then she confesses her vile adultery?

CRANMER: No, but—

*A cannon blast is heard.*

HENRY: No? A good man has just been sent to the grave for her and she denies it? I do not execute my friends for sport, sir. That man's blood sullies her hands, not mine. I have shown more charity than she warrants. I'll not be played for a fool. Now come, to the paper.

CRANMER: But my Lord.

*A second cannon blast is heard.*

HENRY: On with it!

CRANMER: Am I to enter the grounds here, my Lord?

HENRY: Indeed. About it, you bumbling fool.

*They wait while CRANMER writes. JANE tries to diffuse the tension.*

JANE SEYMOUR: Sweet, my lord—

HENRY: PEACE!

JANE SEYMOUR: You have borne her abuse with such patience, my Lord, that I—

HENRY: *(To CRANMER.)* What, have you finished, man?

CRANMER: My Lord, I have.

Richard Hurst (Thomas Cranmer)

HENRY: Then read it out.

CRANMER: Sir?

*Third cannon blast.*

HENRY: READ IT OUT!!!

CRANMER: Certainly. *(He reads.)* Because this marriage was embarked upon for the express purpose of generating an heir to the throne, and because the queen has proven to be bereft of sons, due to the king's lack of manly vigour, and subsequent failure to perform his function as a husband, leaving his true and obedient wife—

HENRY: WHAT?!!

CRANMER: Forgive me, your highness. This was all the grounds she could supply.

HENRY: I'll have your head.

CRANMER: My body and soul are yours to command, my liege.

HENRY: Such lies shall not be entered as evidence.

CRANMER: I have no other grounds to offer.

HENRY: Rubbish, she promised herself to Harry Percy.

CRANMER: She swears she did not.

HENRY: She loved him.

CRANMER: She denies it, and swears she has loved only you.

HENRY: SHE NEVER LOVED ME! The marriage shall be nullified without grounds.

CRANMER: I cannot do that, My Lord.

HENRY: You cannot, hah?

CRANMER: Before God, I must have—

HENRY: "Must" what, mumbling church mouse?

CRANMER: My liege—

HENRY: Your titles can quickly be bestowed upon another after your death.

*A fourth cannon blast sounds.*

CRANMER: As you are the sovereign lord not only of the nation, but of the Church of England, I must suppose that your will is God's will. Therefore if it is God's will that this marriage be annulled without grounds, I shall humbly labour to do His service.

HENRY: Proceed.

CRANMER: I hereby declare the marriage of Henry, the eighth of that name to rule England and Lady Anne Boleyn nullified. Before God this marriage was unlawful and all the issue of this marriage are likewise illegitimate.

HENRY: Look you keep to your house until I have need of you again. Farewell.

CRANMER: God's peace be with you, sire.

HENRY: Come, Mistress.

JANE SEYMOUR: With all obedience to my loving King, I follow.

*JANE and HENRY exit together, CRANMER exits alone.*

**Scene 3: Anne's Chamber**

*ANNE and the FOOL are alone, listening in silence to the cannons. The final cannon blast is heard.*

FOOL: It's done.

ANNE: Don't speak.

FOOL: Must my vow of silence begin now, Madam?

*(Pause.)* Tell me, when we are in Antwerp, shall I be a nun too, or shall I remain your Fool? *(Pause.)* A Fool for nuns. A novel occupation. Perhaps if that grows stale I could become a musician for the deaf, or a painter for the blind: at least there my pains would not earn me censure. *(Pause.)* I wonder that they would even let me through the door; but I suppose if they'll admit one fool why should they not admit two?

ANNE: You needn't come with me.

FOOL: No, it seems I'm welcome to remain here with my Lady Wormwood. Stay or go there's no escaping: I shall be whipped.

ANNE: Five others have been sent to their graves for naught but their association with me. Their bodies not yet cold and you moaning about being whipped.

FOOL: Forgive me, Lady.

*LADY KINGSTON and MISTRESS STONER return unseen by ANNE.*

ANNE: May he burn in hell for all eternity for his—

LADY KINGSTON: Deep in holy contemplation, I see. Won't you make a lovely nun.

*Pause.*

MISTRESS STONER: I would be honoured, Lady, if you would pray with me now.

ANNE: What?

MISTRESS STONER: A prayer for the men: to help their little souls up to heaven.

ANNE: Yes. Yes of course.

LADY KINGSTON: Pfff…

MISTRESS STONER: Your brother died very well, madam. You could just see him reaching out to take the hand of God! You can take some comfort in that.

ANNE: Yes, thank you.

MISTRESS STONER: They're in a better place now, Lady. And you will be soon, too.

ANNE: What?

MISTRESS STONER: Safe in the arms of Jesus.

ANNE: No.

MISTRESS STONER: I mean in Antwerp: in the holy order.

ANNE: Oh yes. Yes, I shall—

LADY KINGSTON: Oh no you shan't. The king will never agree to let you—

ANNE: The king means to spare me! He requested an annulment to nullify the charges of adultery.

LADY KINGSTON: You're a fool. Your marriage was annulled for the benefit of my niece; to publish your child a bastard and clear the way for her issue.

ANNE: Fie!

LADY KINGSTON: The king wants you dead.

ANNE: Send for Cranmer at once. I must speak with him.

LADY KINGSTON: He's locked up for offending the king—

ANNE: But surely he can—

LADY KINGSTON: —and he's not to leave his house until you're dead.

ANNE: Will he deny me the chance to make my last confession and be shriven?

LADY KINGSTON: Howl your confession to the empty air. Burn in hell. Come Mistress Stoner.

MISTRESS STONER: But madam—

LADY KINGSTON: We needn't waste our time with this rubbish.

MISTRESS STONER: Lady Kingston, you may leave if you wish, but I swore to you I would serve our queen unto death and I mean to keep that promise!

FOOL: When did you make that vow?

MISTRESS STONER: Some seven days ago when Lady Kingston asked—

FOOL: She hadn't yet been tried.

MISTRESS STONER: No, but—

ANNE: My death has been assured for a full week?

MISTRESS STONER: Oh no! It's been much longer than that.

FOOL: Yet you said nothing.

MISTRESS STONER: Hope is such a precious thing, Lady. I couldn't take that from you, too.

ANNE: I have been a fool.

FOOL: Not as great a fool as I.

ANNE: Lady Kingston, how long have you been plotting my demise with your wretched niece Mistress Seymour?

FOOL: Seem Whore? No: is Whore. You were the king's whore once, too, weren't you, Lady King's-cunt? In your youth; many many years ago.

ANNE: Have you been the one schooling her in the art of seducing my husband?

LADY KINGSTON: Certainly not, she learned that from you.

ANNE: You shall burn for all eternity!

LADY KINGSTON: I only did what you did to good Queen Catherine. You've created your own fate. Your devastation lies not in a cruel husband or an ambitious rival, but in your own pathetic lack of cunning! And how many others will lose their lives because of your bungling? Five men dead! You might have saved one or two with a strategic and timely confession, but it's too late for aught but regrets now. Cranmer has won the king's displeasure, Thomas Wyatt has been imprisoned. How long will they live, I wonder? And who else will die for you? Your father who pandered his daughters to the king? Your sister and her bastards? Your bastard Elizabeth? Imagine, standing at the gates facing St. Peter, drenched in the blood of everyone who ever dared to love you. I reap such joy thinking about it.

*LADY KINGSTON exits.*

FOOL: And we must all find our joy where we can.

***No Joy***

ANNE: There is no joy in this prison,
Nothing to make it worth the wait.
No happy news comes through those doors,
And nothing can relieve our fate.
We come into this world unfit to survive.
Our cries of rage are met with scant concern.
We suck life from our mothers to stay alive,
And from that first taste of satisfaction we learn:
That appetites exist to be quenched,
And suffering is the lot of those who fail,
And failure is the fate of those whose appetites exceed themselves,
And thus are all the hungry sent to jail.

My hunger taught me ambition.
Ambition taught me to fight.

And victory proves that joy is fleeting,
But suffering reigns all through the night.
So in this prison of our flesh we suffer;
Contentment thwarted by desire's increase.
Like Sisyphus we toil in bootless enterprise,
With no heart to continue, yet in fear of death's release.
My suffering began in the womb.
How can I hope that freedom waits in the tomb?

MISTRESS STONER: Now, lady, you make it worse by thinking so. It's true that suffering can endure for the night, but have you ne'er heard that joy comes in the morning?

ANNE: If there were joy in mourning I should be ecstatic: everyone who has ever loved me is dead. Dead at my hands.

FOOL: There's one who loves you dearly that yet breathes.

ANNE: Sentimental fool, my husband never loved me.

FOOL: It's myself I mean.

ANNE: It's my husband's love I need.

FOOL: If only he had loved you as you loved him. And I had loved you as you have loved me. I would not be contemplating spending the rest of my life in this prison.

ANNE: As am I, but the rest of your life is considerably longer than mine.

FOOL: Yea, my suffering shall be prolonged!

ANNE: You shall shortly be released: learn to be agreeable.

FOOL: No, I lack a talent for flattery. I shall not win my liberty with honeyed words and empty sentiment; promising love that is never given. I cannot feign affection, as others can. I cannot lay down my body

(l to r): Marina Stephenson Kerr (Anne) and Nancy Drake (Fool)

for the pleasure of a man who moves me to naught but revulsion, as others can. I could not sacrifice my own child for selfish ends. As others can. My heart, and not my will, determines my allegiances. And as my heart's foolish subject I followed you here, but as it's wretched slave I shall remain; a fate I scarce deserve.

ANNE: But I deserve to die, is that your drift?

MISTRESS STONER: No one deserves to die Lady, but we all do.

FOOL: What do you have to live for? You love no one, take joy in nothing.

ANNE: That's not true.

FOOL: You had life's treasures laid out before you yet you took no delight. Hoarding future happiness you squandered present joy, and now you die in misery.

MISTRESS STONER: She's not dead yet.

FOOL: She has never lived.

MISTRESS STONER: Pay her no heed, Lady. *(To FOOL.)* Such regrets will serve her but poorly upon the scaffold! Shame on you!

FOOL: She will approach her death as she approached life: in fear and dread, with a bellyful of resentment consuming her, in blind ignorance to the sacrifice of the ones who truly loved her. Who continue, despite all provocation, to love her!

MISTRESS STONER: Lady, you can still choose to die with grace.

*ANNE turns away from them both. The OFFICER enters.*

OFFICER: Forgive me, Lady, I regret I must lead you to your death.

ANNE: Oh heaven help me. I am not fit!

MISTRESS STONER: So soon? It cannot be.

ANNE: No. They must wait. I am not ready. I received no word—

OFFICER: No no no no no. I have not come for the disgraced queen, but for her Fool.

*A brief pause is broken by the FOOL's laughter.*

FOOL: I have deserved hanging ere now. Pray who is having me silenced? Or are you as blissfully ignorant as you were before?

OFFICER: No, Madam. I've a new post now.

FOOL: And snappy new togs to boot!

OFFICER: Not just that: heaps more responsibility. I'm working here now, for Lord Kingston, though to speak true I ought to say I'm working for her Ladyship. She's the one put this charge of insubordination on you.

FOOL: I'm being hanged for insubordination?

OFFICER: She says you're incorrigible.

FOOL: Don't doubt it.

*The OFFICER moves to put cuffs on the FOOL.*

ANNE: Hold, please, sir.

FOOL: Forgive me, madam.

ANNE: Forgive me, Fool.

FOOL: I am wrong to blame you: naught but my love for you brought me here, and I alone must bear the blame for following a foolish heart.

ANNE: I don't deserve your love.

FOOL: No one deserves to be loved, but fools still answer the call.

ANNE: You should not have heeded it.

FOOL: And live a traitor to my profession?

ANNE: Now you die for your folly.

FOOL: I'll die for love, which is the same thing.

ANNE: You don't deserve to hang.

FOOL: You insult me; am I not a fool?

ANNE: You should not die. It's wrong!

FOOL: It is as it should be. Courage. *(They embrace.)* Farewell, Mistress Stoner.

MISTRESS STONER: Oh you're a right good fool!

FOOL: Give the lady honest counsel.

MISTRESS STONER: I shall strive to honour your memory.

FOOL: Now now, none of that. Come sirrah, before the ladies haul out their hankies. Goodnight, good ladies!

*The OFFICER and the FOOL make to exit.*

ANNE: Farewell, Fool.

*The FOOL turns back.*

FOOL: Anne.

ANNE: What?

FOOL: My name. My name is Anne, like you.

ANNE: Anne.

FOOL: I thought someone should know. *(To the OFFICER.)* Incorrigible, you say? Perhaps I shall mount the scaffold snarling and spitting; give the people a good show!

*The OFFICER and the FOOL exit.*

MISTRESS STONER: You have been sorely wronged, Lady.

ANNE: No. No. I am what she says I am. A stranger to my own heart; bitter and joyless. I never loved her. I never loved my husband nor my child. I never loved.

MISTRESS STONER: Oh heavens, no.

ANNE: I deserve to burn in hell.

MISTRESS STONER: Of course you do, so do we all. Here, *(Offering ANNE the flask.)* a drop of comfort.

*ANNE drinks.*

ANNE: It's like the flames of hell in my throat.

MISTRESS STONER: Only at first. Soon enough you'll feel the warmth of God's love spreading in your belly.

ANNE: I am vile.

MISTRESS STONER: You are a child of God.

When I see a man about to die, no matter what vile thing he's done, if he dies with grace he looks to me like Jesus at his final moment, and oh, I just fall in love with our saviour all over again! A man who could look through the windows of your eyes to the stains on your soul and still say "I love you".

ANNE: No one could ever look at me so.

MISTRESS STONER: A man on the scaffold, or a woman for that matter, facing her death, will look at her worst enemy with the purest love. If she dies with grace, that is.

ANNE: And if she cannot? Will she— must she—

MISTRESS STONER: A child will fall when learning to walk and the nurse will help her up and kiss her tears away. You'll not be punished for falling. You're just learning, my love.

ANNE: I am so afraid.

MISTRESS STONER: Be brave.

ANNE: I don't feel brave. I feel scared.

MISTRESS STONER: That's what bravery feels like.

***Hush Now***

MISTRESS STONER: Hush now, my pretty one, it's over.
Lay your burden down.
Your worried head rest upon my soft breast.
Soon you'll be safe in the ground.
And the flowers will grow,
So the whole world will know
That you did your best to be brave and strong.
From the moment of your birth,
'Til you're cradled in the earth,
All we can do is hold on.

## Scene 4: The Chapel

*HENRY and JANE enter the chapel. They attempt to play their game of temptation/flirtation, but it's getting old and somewhat bitter.*

JANE SEYMOUR: Here we are again, and once again your archbishop is late.

HENRY: Not late at all. I've brought you here early to try again your honour.

JANE SEYMOUR: Will you never give up?

HENRY: I wonder that of you, my lady. What more can I do to prove myself? To demonstrate the honour of my intentions? I think you do not love me.

JANE SEYMOUR: My sovereign lord, my love for you o'ersways my virtue, which advises me to shun these assignations. I fear I shall betray my passionate heart. I must wear a mask of cold indifference for I fain would let you know my true desire.

HENRY: *(Dropping all artifice.)* Do you love me?

JANE SEYMOUR: What?!

HENRY: Tell me true.

JANE SEYMOUR: My lord, I …

HENRY: No of course not.

JANE SEYMOUR: I love you, Henry.

HENRY: Truly?

JANE SEYMOUR: With all my heart!

HENRY: Oh yes! Oh you wonder! And do you desire me as I desire you?

JANE SEYMOUR: With the same fervent desperation.

HENRY: Oh Jane, oh my love: breathe your desires into mine ear.

JANE SEYMOUR: My desires?

HENRY: Tell me how you would love me.

JANE SEYMOUR: I know nothing of the ways of—

HENRY: Throw off this mask of cold indifference, love! Tell me how you desire to be touched.

JANE SEYMOUR: Against my better judgment, I yield to your beseeching.

*She whispers in his ear.*

HENRY: Oh… Oh… Touch me, darling, feel your words' effect.

*He forces her hand to his privates. She resists.*

JANE SEYMOUR: I dare not. What then would you think of me?

HENRY: Let not your virtue make you hoard your love.

*He holds her.*

JANE SEYMOUR: Ugh!

HENRY: Love is virtuous.

*She struggles.*

JANE SEYMOUR: Please, sir.

HENRY: No no no, don't be afraid!

JANE SEYMOUR: Stop it now!

HENRY: Let me touch your breast, so soft and fair.

JANE SEYMOUR: Please!

HENRY: You have aroused my passion!

JANE SEYMOUR: Please, sir stop.

HENRY: Let me have you.

JANE SEYMOUR: No!

*She breaks away and falls to her knees.*

I beg your forgiveness. It is unkind of me to lay the burden of my chastity upon your virtue to protect, whiles I wantonly arouse your desire. But I swear when I am married, my body I'll lay down before my lord to use as it would please his heart, unworthy as I am to be so honoured.

*HENRY walks with intent towards JANE. CRANMER enters.*

HENRY: Look who comes to greet us, my Lady. At liberty to walk abroad despite his great offense to our honour. You see what a merciful and generous sovereign is your beloved?

JANE SEYMOUR: Your charitable nature has long been admired by me.

HENRY: Get up, miss, you may finish your prayers another time.

JANE SEYMOUR: Yes, thank you. Good morrow, Father.

CRANMER: God smile upon you Lady, and upon your highness.

HENRY: Archbishop Cranmer, know you why I have sent for you, on this of all days?

CRANMER: My Lord, I do not.

HENRY: Ha! But were you to hazard a guess, what would you say?

CRANMER: Perhaps it could be something touching the conclusion on this day of a most unhappy chapter of your life.

HENRY: Unhappy chapter? What mean you? Speak plain.

CRANMER: My lord, today Anne Boleyn shall, by your order, be put to the sword.

HENRY: By my order?

CRANMER: For crimes unspeakable committed against your gracious person.

HENRY: Thomas.

CRANMER: Yes, my liege?

HENRY: Do you take me for the sort of man who wastes his time with vain regrets?

CRANMER: Certainly not, my Lord.

HENRY: No?

CRANMER: No, you are a forward thinking and…progressive monarch.

HENRY: Yes?

CRANMER: Your vision and leadership in enacting religious reforms in this country speak not only to your deep devotion to God, but also to your commitment to the people of England, among whom I count myself the least worthy of your favour.

HENRY: The very least.

CRANMER: We…we are fortunate indeed, to be blessed with…the visionary ruler we have in you… And I would argue it is your continued devotion to God which bestows such powers of greatness in you to be…unerring…infallible, one might say—

HENRY: Infallible! Very good. And as a man who looks to the future with hope and optimism, as any great visionary must, I have called you here not to mourn the passing of woe, but to clear the way for future happiness.

CRANMER: With joyful obedience, I look to your command.

HENRY: Then cast aside all thoughts of she who is to die today. Think not on her.

CRANMER: My thoughts are yours to command.

HENRY: Brilliant. Now, to my future joy. It is my purpose to be wed to this most virtuous maid.

CRANMER: And England is the richer for the match.

HENRY: We shall be married within the month.

CRANMER: It shall be my honour to bless this union.

HENRY: Bless it now. In earnest of future solemnities.

CRANMER: Eternal God, send thy blessing upon these thy

servants as they pledge themselves to each other. May they ever live in perfect love together. Amen.

HENRY: What say you, miss? Now, afore God, you are mine.

JANE SEYMOUR: I thank your highness for this honour, bestowed on one as undeserving as myself.

HENRY: Come with me to my chamber, at last we can celebrate the joy of this contract together.

JANE SEYMOUR: But we are merely betrothed, my lord.

HENRY: Fear not. As you are mine, I am yours, spoken before a priest in a house of God. Come, miss…

JANE SEYMOUR: Good my Lord, my modesty forbids—

HENRY: If your modesty forbids your husband, you are not his wife.

CRANMER: Lady, do you wish to be this good man's wife?

JANE SEYMOUR: Oh yes! Yes, truly.

CRANMER: Then, madam, I must counsel you to obey your husband's will. Your modesty must bend to suit the time, or you dishonour yourself, your king and your country.

JANE SEYMOUR: *(Kneels and kisses his ring.)* I thank you reverend sir.

CRANMER: I am your servant.

*She doesn't rise, so he kneels with her.*

It is not given to us to amend what is amiss, but to quietly suffer what we cannot change. Look up clear. Go to your Lord.

JANE SEYMOUR: *(She does.)* Sir, in loving obedience I submit to bend my will to your highness' pleasure.

HENRY: Ha! Saucy lass! Farewell Thomas.

CRANMER: God's benediction on your betrothal.

*HENRY and JANE exit.*

***Confession Song***

CRANMER: Tomorrow she will come for confession,
Shivering 'neath a blanket of shame,
And I shall offer her redemption,
In God and King Henry's holy name.
It never gets easier, I've heard it all before,
Sacrificed to a sadist, the virgin becomes the whore.
And I confess I have become King Henry's bawd,
I've bent the holy word to suit his pleasure,
I have demeaned my soul's most precious treasure,
Slave to my king, but stranger to my God.
But now upon my knees and from my soul,
I ask you, if you can, to make me whole.

*JANE enters in a state of distress and undress.*

JANE SEYMOUR: Now I confess I feel like I've somehow been cheated,
This isn't what I expected at all!
Stripped and flung about like a rag doll.
And though I've won, I feel I've been defeated.
I thought I had it all under control,
But now I pray to God to make me whole.

*HENRY enters.*

HENRY: Now I confess I hate this desperate beastly act.
No self-respecting woman could submit
To bear the weight of passion's frenzied fit
And hold her own integrity intact.
Into this whore I pour the essence of my soul.
Restore my dignity, dear God, and make me whole.

CRANMER: Now I confess I've whored myself for Henry's sake.

JANE SEYMOUR: This all has been a terrible mistake.

CRANMER: And God alone knows how I've been forsworn.

JANE SEYMOUR: I thought I wanted this but I'm forlorn.

TOGETHER: But now upon my knees and from my soul
I beg you, if you can, to make me whole.

HENRY: I like the wooing and the courting,
All the flirting and the sporting,
And the rush of spirit's shuddering release.
But this nonsense in between
Where we're both of us demeaned,
Panting like two sordid rutting beasts…
Now I confess I hate this desperate beastly act.

CRANMER: An act of love.

JANE SEYMOUR: I'm not sure how I should react.

HENRY: But England will be weak without an heir.

CRANMER: To err is human.

JANE SEYMOUR: Oh I am sick at heart, I am in despair.

TOGETHER: For power I have sacrificed my soul.
I don't think even God can make me whole.

**Scene 5: Anne's Chamber**

*ANNE is illuminated kneeling, the others fade to black. The song continues.*

ANNE: I confess…
I confess…
I confess…
I confess I tried my best.
I confess that my best was insufficient.
And all my efforts ended up deficient.
Now I confess I failed at everything I tried,
For fruitless honours I cheated and I lied.

I failed to trust in providence divine,
But like a desp'rate beggar clung to what was mine.
Despising God's creation with each breath,
Bereft of grace I now must face my death.
I hate myself, my sallow, bloodstained soul:
And though I don't deserve it,
I don't deserve it but I beg you if you can,
For the nothing that I am,
Let me know
What it feels like to be whole.

*The light spreads and MISTRESS STONER enters with hairpins.*

MISTRESS STONER: Here we are. *(She stands behind ANNE, arranging her hair.)* Now let me pin it up for you, just to get it up off your neck. A nice clean blow, that's what you want; no impediments. I can't tell you what a bollocks they make of it when the hair gets in the way. Don't try to argue that it looks better down, this is no time for vanity!

ANNE: Yes.

MISTRESS STONER: Such lovely hair you have: very pretty.

ANNE: Thank you.

MISTRESS STONER: He must have loved your hair.

ANNE: Who?

MISTRESS STONER: The king. I think he must have very much admired your beautiful hair.

ANNE: Yes, I believe he did.

MISTRESS STONER: He did his best, love.

ANNE: Yes, I know.

MISTRESS STONER: *(She finishes with her hair.)* And there you are; all ready to go. Yes?

ANNE: Yes.

*KINGSTON enters.*

KINGSTON: Lady, I regret I must lead you to the scaffold.

ANNE: Thank you, Lord Kingston, I am ready to die.

*LADY KINGSTON enters.*

LADY KINGSTON: The crowd is eager to see it.

ANNE: They shan't be disappointed.

LADY KINGSTON: No they shall not. What a pity you won't be alive to hear them cheering, isn't it? As your head hits the dirt. You've only yourself to blame, you filthy, usurping whore.

*ANNE looks at LADY KINGSTON. LADY KINGSTON is shamed and exits.*

KINGSTON: You must forgive my wife, your majesty. She wasn't always thus, but she has found marriage rather a disappointment.

ANNE: A common complaint nowadays. But I assure you, she has no cause, sir.

KINGSTON: This way, your majesty.

*ANNE approaches the scaffold where the SWORDSMAN awaits her.*

MISTRESS STONER: Oh my heart, there he is. Isn't he lovely!

ANNE: I hear he is very good. And I have a little neck. Mistress Stoner?

MISTRESS STONER: Madam?

ANNE: Don't turn away.

MISTRESS STONER: What?

ANNE: Be brave.

*ANNE mounts the scaffold and addresses the assembled onlookers.*

Good people. I am come hither to die, for according to the law, I am judged to die, and therefore will I speak nothing against it. I am come hither to accuse no man. But I pray to God to save the King and send him long to reign over you, for a gentler nor a more merciful prince was there never: and to me he was ever a good, a gentle and sovereign Lord. And thus I take my leave of the world, and of you all, and I heartily desire you all to pray for me.

*ANNE kneels and looks to MISTRESS STONER.*

ANNE: Are you ready?

MISTRESS STONER: Off you go.

*ANNE gives the signal to the SWORDSMAN. He raises his blade. ANNE is suddenly isolated in light.*

ANNE: Such clarity I feel. And I can see all things at once, yet nothing's jumbled. All my days, my triumphs and woes, my loves and fears. And all the people: the ones who've gone before beckon me to join them. And, look; the ones who haven't yet been awaiting their turn, like pretty ladies at a dance. And all the ones here now. *(To audience.)* Look at you! All you beautiful people, shining with love, nursing secret regrets, holding back, saving something, giving too much, feeling foolish, giving up, trying again, filled with desire, waiting for tomorrow… Hello, sweet people. Your time is short. There is only now. This moment. You must be very brave.

*Blackout.*

*The End.*